Swindon

History and Guide

Swindon

History and Guide

John Chandler

ALAN SUTTON

First published in the United Kingdom in 1992 by
Alan Sutton Publishing Ltd
Phoenix Mill · Far Thrupp · Stroud · Gloucestershire

First published in the United States of America in 1992 by
Alan Sutton Publishing Inc. · Wolfeboro Falls · NH 03896-0848

British Library Cataloguing in Publication Data

Chandler, John H.
Swindon: History and Guide
I. Title
942.313
ISBN 0-7509-0190-X

Jacket Illustration: The Windmill Estate, Swindon (*Paul Felix*)

For Roger Trayhurn, in recognition of more than twenty-five
years' distinguished service to the people of Swindon and their
history.

Typeset in 10/13 Times.
Typesetting and origination by
Alan Sutton Publishing Limited.
Printed in Great Britain by
The Bath Press, Avon.

Contents

1. Swindon Landscapes   1

2. But a Small Place   14

3. The First Push   26

4. A God of Steam   41

5. Brick-Built Breeding Boxes   57

6. Evening Star and Sunrise   72

Walking Tour: Old and New Swindon   87

The Next Steps   112

Acknowledgements   117

Picture Credits   118

Index   119

Swindon Landscapes

windon is best approached from the south. Driving up from Devizes, after many miles of downland the traveller begins to descend, and a different world suddenly reveals itself. Beyond the flat green patchwork of Wroughton's rectangular fields and the incessant motorway there are houses and factories, office blocks and warehouses, a church spire and a hospital. From my vantage point parked in the lay-by where the view begins I am watching Swindon wake up. It is seven o'clock on a spring morning, and the sun is dissolving a light lingering mist in preparation for another hot day. With binoculars I can make out the hazy outline of higher ground, the Corallian ridge on which Purton, Blunsdon and Stratton are perched, and I can see that in places the houses extend up to and over this temporary horizon. Later the mist will clear, to reveal Braydon Forest and the Cotswolds beyond. In front of me a broad low hill rises from the valley to mask the longer view; it was this limestone eminence which gave Swindon its name, and it was here that Old Swindon, or High Swindon, was built. To its right I can make out more offices and factories, and I know that behind them is rolled a carpet of houses far further than the eye can see.

Of the many hundreds of buildings discernible through the mist perhaps only a dozen are more than 150 years old, and they are almost all outside Swindon, at Wroughton and Elcombe in the foreground. Away to my left Toothill, Freshbrook and the other West Swindon neighbourhoods have all arrived since I occasionally used to cycle along there to work from Wootton Bassett seventeen years ago. Swindon itself had a population below 2,000 until about 1840; now, including Stratton, it is approaching 150,000. Perhaps, therefore, this book should begin in 1840.

But that would be quite wrong. The landscape itself, on which modern Swindon so recently sits, has been shaped and modified by men and women since prehistory, and here and there (and more than most

Opposite: Swindon glimpsed from the Devizes road as it descends the chalk hillside south of Wroughton.

people imagine) traces of their handiwork show through. This chapter examines the landscapes of greater Swindon, from their geological origins through centuries of agriculture and rural settlement, up to the point at which they became 'Swindonized'. In chapters two and three we shall look at the successive communities which have lived at the heart of these landscapes, on Swindon Hill itself; and from chapter four onwards we shall enter the world of railways, suburbs and urban life generally, the Swindon which we know today.

Southern England's terrain results from a sequence of rocks formed as sediment on the ocean floor. The chemical composition of each stratum depends on various factors, including the nature of the river-borne material being carried into the ocean at the time, and the organisms which the water could sustain. Geological forces have buckled the strata, and climatic forces have eroded them, so that different rocks surface in different places, and have succumbed in various ways to the effects of water, frost and vegetation. A line drawn on a map across the Swindon area, from Chiseldon in the south-east to Cricklade in the north-west, represents a journey back through geological time, as different rocks are encountered, each older than the one before. The downland above Chiseldon and Wroughton, where I am sitting, is made of chalk, the youngest rock in the sequence. Below this chalk the line traverses greensands and clays, then the Corallian limestone, then older clays beyond. Because of their different properties the rocks manifest themselves in different ways – the chalk as well-drained rounded hills, the heavy clays as flat valleys, often waterlogged, the limestone as an irregular ridge, and so on.

This over-simplification explains much of the landscape structure seen from the lay-by above Wroughton. But it does not account for Swindon Hill, which at its western limit near Princess Margaret Hospital stands up proud from the clay, and which extends eastwards almost to the chalk beyond Broome. This hill is largely composed of Portland and Purbeck Beds, fine building limestones which occur also in south Wiltshire and Dorset. Their presence here is explained by a syncline, or concave fold, in the clay at this point, which beneath the ocean filled up with deep deposits of shelly sediment. The deposits compacted to form these hard limestones, which are more resistant to weathering than the surrounding clays, and so have been left standing high and dry above the valley.

The underlying geology has determined not only the scenery, but also the vegetation which grows on its soil. The lighter soils of the chalk hillsides and the limestone ridges are better for arable cultivation than the sticky clay, and these must have been heavily exploited for

Opposite: Simplified geology of the Swindon area.

CRICKLADE

HIGHWORTH

BROAD BLUNSDON

BLUNSDON ST ANDREW

Groundwell

Penhill   Kingsdown

Haydon Wick

Mouldon   SOUTH MARSTON

Moredon

Sparcells   RODBOURNE   STRATTON ST MARGARET

LYDIARD MILLICENT   Nythe

Shaw

Wick Farm
LYDIARD TREGOZE

Mannington   Liddington Wick

Toot Hill   SWINDON

Blagrove   WANBOROUGH

                                                  Badbury Wick

Chaddington   LIDDINGTON

                        WROUGHTON

                                          CHISELDON

Clays	Corallian	Portland/Purbeck	Lower Greensand	Gault	Upper Greensand	Chalk

An aerial view of part of Burderop Down, south of Chiseldon. A medieval D-shaped enclosure has been superimposed on boundary banks which survive from a network of small prehistoric enclosed fields (sometimes known as 'Celtic' fields).

growing crops during later prehistory. In general subsequent centuries of farming have obliterated the archaeological evidence, but at the margins left untouched by the medieval plough, such as on Burderop Down below the hillfort at Barbury, a network of small field boundaries survives as earthworks to show just how far up the hillside the prehistoric arable farmer was prepared to go. The claylands provided other resources – woodland for building, fuel and pannage, clay for pottery, and, when cleared, grassland for pasturing cattle.

A glimpse of farming life in the Swindon landscape during the Iron Age has been provided by archaeological discoveries made in 1976–7, when the Groundwell Farm industrial estate was being built. A sequence of four round wooden houses within an enclosure was excavated, together with granaries and other farm buildings. From pottery and animal bone it seemed that this was the working farm of a single family, and was in use from after 500 BC until before 200 BC. Their farming economy was mixed, and combined crop-growing (probably using oxen as draught animals) with the rearing of sheep and pigs. Pig bones were more numerous than on similar sites elsewhere, and this suggests that they were using woodland on the adjacent clays for pannage. The farmers seem to have been quite poor, since few metal implements were in use, and after the house and farmyard had been abandoned for several centuries the site was cleared and put down to

Roman Period.

arable, probably before AD 100. A reconstruction model of Groundwell iron-age farm is displayed in Swindon Museum.

Groundwell was probably typical of many small farms dotted around the Swindon landscape in later prehistory. They came and went, and some, such as the larger settlement recently excavated at Cleveland Farm, Ashton Keynes, continued as native communities during the centuries of Roman occupation. The Saxon place-name 'Walcot', which means something like 'the huts of the natives', may refer to one such settlement, which must have survived beyond the end of the Roman period and still have been in use several centuries later. By their activities, clearing woodland, manuring soil, making and consolidating tracks, building houses and marking out territories, the prehistoric and Roman farmers doubtless modified the landscape in ways which still affect modern Swindon; but how many of our modern roads and administrative boundaries owe their idiosyncrasies to such distant ancestors we shall probably never know.

Apart from the downland hillforts and field systems the oldest tangible pieces of human endeavour in the Swindon area are two Roman roads. Ermin Street, as part of the route from London to Cirencester is known, and another road which ran north from the Roman town at Mildenhall, near Marlborough, to meet it near Covingham, have both been superimposed over parts of their route by the A419 dual carriageway. The topography of Stratton St Margaret is patently dominated by the line of Ermin Street, and this link with Rome is a matter of local pride and folk etymology. 'You know what Stratton means, don't you?' I was once told by an elderly inhabitant, '– straight on!'. The name, which is Saxon, does indeed refer to Ermin Street, but not quite so blatantly: it means 'farm by the paved road'.

Few motorists today, hurrying up the A419 from the Common Head roundabout, probably have time to ponder the fact that the bend in the road's direction from north to north-west is actually caused by the junction of Roman roads, nor that the name of the area to their left, Dorcan, is in fact a distant echo of the small town, *Durocornovium*, which Roman administrators established at that road junction. Part of this settlement was explored between 1966 and 1976, before much of it disappeared under modern road works. The excavations revealed that it included a *mansio*, or official staging-post for Roman soldiers, messengers and other government staff – a kind of motorway service area for the use of pass-holders only. The town which grew up alongside this *mansio* was planned as a grid of streets and aligned on the Roman road. It served not only as an amenity for travellers, but also as a focus for the surrounding countryside, including the whole of the Swindon area.

The countryside around *Durocornovium* included not only the homesteads of small farmers, in the native iron-age mould, but also two other groups who arrived in the wake of Roman prosperity. During the second century potters colonized the claylands and began to produce cooking pots, jars and other coarse pottery for the *Durocornovium* market. Evidence of their kilns was discovered in advance of the West Swindon development (one area has been named Kiln Park to commemorate their work) at various sites between Swindon and Purton, where not only the local clay could be exploited, but also ample woodland for fuel to fire the kilns. The industry, which probably supplied tiles for building as well as domestic pottery, had affinities with other production centres, at Gloucester and in Savernake Forest, but seems only to have flourished for two or three generations.

The other group to emerge around *Durocornovium*, as elsewhere, was a class of sophisticated farmer–landowners, who reorganized local agriculture on the basis of the villa estate. Evidence of Roman villas,

An artist's reconstruction of Roman pottery kilns at Shaw, West Swindon. A potter is at work in the building on the right of the picture, with unfired pots standing on the ground next to him. In the centre a turf-lined kiln is being fired, and to the left pots are being removed from a kiln after firing, to be loaded on to a wagon bound for market at *Durocornovium*. Living quarters, small arable fields, and sheep grazing on Toothill may be seen in the background.

either the structures themselves or the trappings of luxury which accompanied them, have been found in various places around Swindon, including Purton, Stanton Fitzwarren, Chiseldon and elsewhere. The largest known villa complex in the area, and one of the largest in England, lay next to the Roman road at Badbury. It was partially and very inadequately excavated during motorway construction between 1969 and 1971, and was found to have flourished almost throughout the Roman period. It included luxurious living apartments and working buildings spaced across an area of some two hectares, which is now largely beneath motorway junction 15 and its access roads.

The owners of such estates must have formed a powerful local aristocracy, and when the edifice of Roman rule, including their small town, crumbled in the fifth century, they did not immediately disappear. At Badbury, for instance, life under reduced circumstances appears to have continued in the east range of buildings for a considerable time. Some of the landholdings associated with Roman villas may have remained as viable economic units through all the turmoil, only to reappear several hundred years later under Saxon landlords. We learn of the boundaries of such estates from surviving copies of the documents which conveyed them from one owner to another. Moredon, for example, now a Swindon suburb, first makes its appearance on the stage of history in 758, when the king of Wessex granted land there to Malmesbury Abbey. Nearly two centuries later, in 943, Moredon occurs in another charter, this time with a description of its boundaries.

Most of these boundaries can still be traced on the ground. They begin at a place called *Higford*, 'the hay ford', which was probably close to where Cricklade Road now crosses the Rodbourne Stream. This stream, called *Hreod Burna*, 'the reedy brook', still lives up to its Saxon name in places, and the boundary ran west along it as far as its confluence with the River Ray (near the site of Moredon power station). Next we can follow it north down the river to Tadpole Lane (by the station on the Swindon to Cricklade railway), then running east along the hedgerows of Tadpole Farm to the sewage works by Lady Lane; from there it was marked by what the charter calls 'an old ditch' as far as the foot of Penhill. After this it turned south, and tracing it among the houses of Haydon Wick and Pinehurst becomes more difficult. At some point it crossed the *Bradan Weg*, or 'wide way', which is presumably the modern Whitworth Road, and the name has been kept in use by the nearby road, Broadway.

Moredon's boundary charter is one of several relating to places around Swindon which have survived. Others describe Purton,

Saxon boundaries of Moredon.

Badbury, Wanborough and part of Wroughton. Doubtless many more once existed which now are lost, setting out in meticulous detail the twists and turns of Swindon's ancient boundaries. To the historian the survivors are important for two reasons. In the first place they offer a kind of bridge between the territories of prehistory and the villa-owners on the one hand, and the later parishes and administrative units on the other, which have in turn shaped the development of towns like Swindon. In the second place they are repositories of Saxon place-names – often the direct ancestors of the modern names in daily use – which are themselves little capsules of information about Saxon landscape, people and settlements.

Familiar names which first occur in documents more than a thou-sand years ago include Groundwell ('the deep spring') and Chiseldon ('the gravel valley'). Three others – Moredon, Mannington and Ellendun – include the Saxon name element *dun*, which means 'hill' or 'high ground', whilst Lydiard and Penhill probably embody much older, Celtic, words for 'ridge' and 'promontory' respectively. At least ten other place-names around Swindon, including Swindon itself, are first recorded in Domesday Book in 1086, although they are likely by then to have been in use already for many years. Other names, not found until documents proliferate in the thirteenth century, were probably also first coined several centuries before. Most seem to be telling us about their position relative to the geological differences of limestone, chalk and clay which we explored earlier. Thus a row of *dun* names is sprinkled along the Corallian ridge – Mouldon, Moredon, Haydon, Blunsdon, Kingsdown – whereas several clayland names suggest waterlogged or wooded conditions; they include Nythe ('land surrounded by water') and South Marston ('farm in the marsh') east of Swindon, and Shaw ('wood'), Sparcells ('wood for spears or spars') and Blagrove ('black thicket') to the west. Mannington (possibly 'Mehha's hill'), Chaddington ('Ceatta's hill') and Toothill ('the lookout hill') all seem to refer to minor eminences rising from the clay. The derivation of Swindon, 'the hill where pigs are kept', is well known, and refers of course to the limestone ridge on which Old Town sits.

We may have noticed, when exploring the Saxon estate of Moredon, 'the hill of waste land', that the name of one prominent feature had already been used to denote the whole territory, even though much of it lay alongside sluggish rivers and among sticky wood pasture, for which 'Moredon' was a quite inappropriate description. When in Domesday Book we find the name Swindon for the first time it had likewise come to be used for a considerable area, embracing in fact much of the large medieval parish, and consisting of five or six distinct landholdings. Thus separate names came into use for some of its constituent parts, such as Eastcott, Westcott and Nethercott ('the eastern, western and lower groups of cottages'), as well as the tautological Even Swindon. This literally means 'the hill of pigs on the flat ground', but of course in reality denotes 'the flat area of the Swindon estate'. By the thirteenth century, when Even Swindon is first recorded, we also find the expression 'High Swindon' in use to describe the area on the hill.

Around the time of Domesday Book the old Saxon estates became bound up with new territorial creations, the ecclesiastical parishes. The modern Swindon conurbation embraces most of three ancient parishes – Swindon itself, Rodbourne Cheney, and Stratton St Margaret – and has in recent years nibbled away at the clayland holdings of several others, such as Liddington, Wroughton and the Lydiards. A parish might include several landholdings or manors – often the successors of Saxon estates – and the subsequent history and ownership of

HIC:EST:VVAD AR/D:

'Here is Wadard', the Bayeux Tapestry tells us, and depicts him riding to Hastings to forage for food after landing on English soil in 1066. Twenty years later, when Domesday Book was compiled, he was a tenant of the Bishop of Bayeux (who commissioned the tapestry) on one of the Swindon estates, known as Nethercott.

Swindon's Domesday manors has been meticulously traced. Their evolution need not concern us too much here, although we shall see in chapter five how, even as late as the 1870s, manorial divisions had a crucial effect on determining where and when Swindon could expand. But two other topics on which manorial history impinges, medieval settlements and agriculture, do demand our attention at this point.

Evidence from archaeology, manorial records and medieval tax lists enables us to build up a picture of where people were living around Swindon and how they were supporting themselves. The larger and more prosperous communities were those to be found on the chalk slopes or the limestone ridge. Here, at places such as Chiseldon, Wanborough, Stratton and Blunsdon, villages were established which have continued to the present day. Several of these hillside villages, in addition to their fields of good arable land on chalky or sandy soil, possessed areas of clay vale which they attempted to exploit as pasture grounds. The name-element *wic* often denotes a secondary settlement or farmstead devoted to dairying, and so we find Haydon Wick, Badbury Wick, Liddington Wick (now beneath the Eldene estate), and Wick Farm at West Swindon (formerly belonging to Lydiard Millicent) all down on the clay below their parent communities. Swindon's own satellite hamlets on the claylands were probably little more than single farmsteads. In 1377 only forty-five adult taxpayers lived in the combined territory of Eastcott, Westcott and Walcot, and another twenty-seven in Even Swindon. These figures compare with 248 on Swindon Hill and 160 at Stratton St Margaret.

The fourteenth century was in general a time of retrenchment and shrinking population after many generations of growth. Among the poorer communities in the Swindon area some, such as Rodbourne Cheney and Even Swindon, managed to continue, whilst others, including Groundwell (with eleven taxpayers in 1377) and Moredon (with sixteen) came near to extinction. Mannington survived until the late fifteenth century, but was then deserted, and its cornfields were converted to sheep pasture. Grassy mounds denoted the position of the villagers' dwellings, and corrugations of ridge and furrow in the fields their acre strips of arable, until everything disappeared beneath the onslaught of West Swindon during the 1980s. Another community, which farmed part of

An aerial photograph of the earthwork remains of the medieval hamlet of Westleaze, which lay south of Swindon Hill. The site is between Princess Margaret Hospital and the motorway.

Wroughton's claylands below Okus, is now represented only by the earthworks and boundary banks of a former village street running from Westleaze to Westleaze Farm, just north of the motorway.

The parish of Swindon in the Middle Ages was divided between five manors, and each appears to have had its own farming regime. On the southern and eastern edges of the parish were the small manors of Broome and Walcot, and occupying Swindon Hill itself and its southern slope was the most productive of the estates, known as High or West Swindon. It included a very large arable field on the hilltop, which was later exploited also by the quarries, together with pasture grounds on the hillside. The two remaining manors, known as East Swindon and Nethercott (which included Eastcott and Westcott) consisted largely of clayland, but each extended some distance up Swindon Hill, on the north and east sides, to benefit from the lighter, more easily worked soils.

Both these poorer, sparsely populated manors attempted to grow crops during the middle ages in open fields on the unsympathetic clay

Part of an Ordnance Survey map published at a scale of one inch to one mile in 1828, based on surveys of the Swindon area begun between 1811 and 1818. The canals are recent arrivals.

soil of the valley; but during the seventeenth century they converted much of their land to enclosed pasture. The enclosure in 1657 of Eastcott manor (as Nethercott had by this time become known) was the subject of a long legal agreement between the various freeholders. This begins by reciting the various difficulties which the farmers were facing. It tells us that the grounds and premises, 'had for a long time past remained much impoverished and decayed by reason of the unaptness of the tillable grounds for corne and grain, which were more apt for grass and hay'. The disorders and inconveniences of the existing regime, it continues, 'could not heretofore be reformed by the reason of the disagreement and wilfulness of some of the inhabitants and occupiers of land there, and by reason of the diversities of tenures and estates, and the said grounds and premises so lying open and dispersed'. Accordingly the old common fields and meadows were divided up, and allotted in blocks to the various freeholders. This process of enclosure imprinted on the landscape many of the lines which, two centuries later, would constrain and be respected by the brand new streets and terraces of New Swindon.

The first Ordnance Survey map of the Swindon area, published in 1828, depicts a world far removed from that of fifty or a hundred years later. From the little foursquare hilltop town westwards to Lydiard, northwards to Blunsdon and eastwards to Wanborough stretch mile after mile of flat countryside, traversed by meandering streams and wandering lanes, and punctuated only by occasional isolated farms. Their names – Westcott, Penhill, Toothill, Walcot, Nythe – are entirely familiar to present-day Swindonians, but their surroundings are not. This older Swindon landscape has been almost completely forgotten, yet it underpins the entire structure and layout of the modern town.

But a Small Place

S windon is a market town, placed on an eminence, which affords an extensive prospect over some parts of Gloucestershire and Berkshire. The pleasantness of its situation, combined with other circumstances, have induced many persons of independent fortune to fix their residence at Swindon; and their mansions contribute as much to ornament the town as their social intercourse may be said to animate and enliven it. To this may be attributed, perhaps, that liberality of mind which now appears to characterise the inhabitants of this little town.' So wrote the topographer and antiquary John Britton, in part of his work about the 'beauties' of Wiltshire which was published in 1825. By Swindon, of course, he meant Old Swindon – New Swindon did not then exist – and it is the evolution of settlement on Swindon Hill leading up to this plateau of Regency decorum which concerns us in the present chapter.

Stray finds of prehistoric artefacts, as well as archaeological work prior to new building, are developing a picture of intermittent human settlement on the hill from the time of nomadic mesolithic hunters and foragers through to the period of Roman colonization from *Durocornovium*. But prehistoric evidence here, generally in the form of flintwork, pits and burials, is really no more than might be expected on any tract of open, fertile, well drained and defensible land such as the hill during prehistory is presumed to have been.

Nor is it any surprise to find that astute Roman farmers and villa-owners also settled here. Nearly a century ago a local antiquary, Arthur Passmore, excavated part of what was probably a villa in the Okus area, and he also found evidence of a Roman building on the northern slope of the hill in what is now Queen's Park. Roman wells, ditches and building materials have subsequently been uncovered between Broome Manor and Coate. A fourth area of Roman activity on the hill, which was excavated in 1975–6, is perhaps the most important, because the site, a short distance due east of Old Swindon's market square, has yielded evidence from both earlier and later periods, as well as two phases of Roman buildings. The second Roman phase consisted of a rough stone-built structure, which could be dated from pottery and coins to the fourth century, not long before the break-down of Roman rule. It replaced an earlier timber building on the site, and was in turn replaced by two small early Saxon huts.

These modest structures are perhaps the links in a chain which connects Roman *Durocornovium* with medieval Swindon and modern Old Town. We know that the community centred on *Durocornovium* was quarrying stone from Swindon Hill for some of its buildings, and there appears to have been a road leading up to the quarries from the Roman town. We also know that the position of *Durocornovium*, dictated by the junction of the Roman roads, was far from ideal. Damp and flooding were clearly troubling the inhabitants, as some buildings there were raised above ground level, rather like granaries on staddle stones, and the problem may have been made worse by a deteriorating climate at the end of the Roman period. It has been suggested that the late Roman and early Saxon discoveries at Old Town perhaps represent a shift away from *Durocornovium* to a more viable site on the hill.

Not far away from where the Roman building had been buried a much larger Saxon hut, nearly nine metres long, was discovered. Its walls had been constructed of wattle and daub, and much of the daub, preserving the impression of the woven wattle structure, had survived the fire which ended the building's career during the middle Saxon period. Beneath the daub were some of the hut's contents, including a

Loomweights used to tension the warp threads during weaving, discovered by archaeological excavation where they had fallen during the fire which destroyed the Saxon weaving hut at Old Swindon.

shelf of pots and the remains of a loom and other weaving equipment. Like other Saxon huts discovered nearby its floor was below ground level, a characteristic of buildings of the sixth and seventh centuries. Another excavation carried out in 1977 behind Lloyd's Bank in Swindon High Street uncovered the same sequence of late prehistoric and Roman settlement beneath a Saxon sunken hut, which had also been used for clothmaking.

Conjectural medieval town plan.

Thus some kind of Saxon hamlet or village existed close to the centre of the later Swindon. The large weaving hut had later buildings superimposed upon it, which dated from the late Saxon and early medieval periods. But their alignment seemed to bear no relationship to the modern street plan. Indeed, more recent investigation detected a possible east–west street running across the line of the later High Street. It is probable, therefore, that between the middle Saxon period and the twelfth or thirteenth century either there was a break in occupation or else a wholesale reorganisation of the settlement took place.

A likely context for any reorganisation of Swindon would have been an attempt to establish a market in about 1260, and so to turn the existing village into a small town. The archaeology so far described suggests that the earlier settlement may have been located to the east of the present High Street. Another clue to its position may be provided by the ruined church of Holy Rood next to the remains of the Goddard family's mansion now known as the Lawn, and close to the site of a mill. Although by all accounts an undistinguished building, the church was said to have incorporated a Norman column; this, together with a twelfth-century reference to a church at Swindon, suggests that it existed long before the market was set up. The mill is thought to have been the successor of one of the two at Swindon recorded in Domesday Book, and the Lawn is believed to occupy the site of its medieval predecessor. Their position therefore, some 300 m east of Swindon High Street, tends to confirm the archaeological testimony.

If all these suppositions are correct then the present street layout of Old Town is likely to have been a planned addition tacked on to the western edge of an already existing village. Certainly the long, narrow strips known as burgage tenements running back from High Street and Wood Street suggest deliberate planning, and the expansionist mid-thirteenth century was exactly the right time for such a development. Similar urban extensions to existing villages occurred in many parts of England, and were common in Wiltshire between about 1210 and 1260. Sherston, Lacock and Market Lavington, to name but three, acquired markets and burgage tenure at this time.

The earliest deed preserved among the archives of the Goddard family (WRO.1461/1) dates from 1346, and records the sale of a tenement in Newport Street.

Many so-called towns created in this way never developed into proper towns in the modern sense, and their medieval status could more accurately be described as that of urban villages. Indeed the three Wiltshire examples chosen have all been regarded for centuries just as large villages. In precisely the same way the medieval town of Swindon must not be overestimated.

The evidence for its urban career is remarkably slight. It seems not to have acquired a proper market charter during the middle ages and, were it not for a complaint by Marlborough tradesmen in 1274 that they had been suffering competition during the fifteen years past from an unofficial market in Swindon, we should have no idea when it began. There are, it is true, occasional references in medieval documents to a market and to burgages; there is by 1346 the appearance of the name Newport Street ('newport' means 'the new market'); and from 1289 Swindon was sometimes called 'Chipping' or 'Market Swindon'. An excavation in 1988 uncovered evidence of a possible boundary wall and wooden building in use in the fourteenth century on the corner of Devizes Road and Britannia Place; this is the first indication to be discovered that the town's built-up area extended as far westwards as Devizes Road.

But the total absence of information about market trading and organization until the seventeenth century, the failure to secure a market charter until 1626, or to develop any kind of guild or corporate government – all are indications that medieval Swindon remained essentially a larger-than-average agricultural community, with perhaps a little quarrying as a sideline, and possibly a few more tradesmen and specialist craftsmen than its neighbours, but that its career as a town had scarcely begun.

Part of a document of 1626 granting to members of the Goddard family the right to hold a weekly market and two annual fairs at Swindon (WRO. 1461/15).

Writing in the 1670s John Aubrey, the Wiltshire intellectual, attributed a rise in Swindon's fortunes during the previous thirty or so years to two factors, its market and its quarries. The market, he explained, had benefited from outbreaks of plague before, and probably after, the civil war. These disrupted normal marketing, and frightened cattle-dealers away from their usual centre at Highworth. Swindon, with its Monday market recently placed on a new and legitimate footing by the 1626 royal charter, appears to have taken and retained some of Highworth's trade. The civil war, too, was bad for Highworth. The town was garrisoned by royalist soldiers, who appear to have intimidated local graziers attending the market; in consequence they moved their business to Swindon.

Aubrey also claimed that the Purbeck limestone, for which the town had become famous by the time that he was writing, was discovered in about 1640, only 5 ft below ground. Stone from Swindon Hill had been exploited, as we have seen, in Roman times, and doubtless supplied local needs during the middle ages. There is a reference to stone slates being taken from Swindon to Sevenhampton in 1301, and an old quarry is referred to in deeds from 1641. But it was during the seventeenth century that Swindon stone acquired a reputation, not only for its smoothness and whiteness when used internally, but also for its resistance to damp. It was in demand during the rebuilding of London after the fire in 1666, and Aubrey implies that carriage was overland to Lechlade and then down the Thames. Certainly quarrymen begin to

Opposite: Part of an Ordnance Survey plan of 1886 showing active and former quarries on Swindon Hill. Much of the area shown was landscaped to become the Town Gardens in 1894.

figure in Swindon manorial records from about 1670, both when they wished to purchase leases of lands for quarrying, and when they fell foul of authority for leaving excavations unfenced, to the danger of travellers.

Aubrey's impression of Swindon on the increase during the seventeenth century is undoubtedly correct, and other sources of information help us to quantify the town's progress. During the eighty years prior to 1640 the new owners of High Swindon, the Goddard family, appear to have made only very modest progress. In 1563 their estate included sixty houses and forty cottages; by 1640 this housing stock had increased by a mere eight, suggesting a rough total population on their manor at both dates of 400–50. During the 1640s there were at least thirty families on the other main Swindon manor, Eastcott, and probably a few others at Walcot and Broome, so we should perhaps add 150–200 to give an approximate total population of Swindon parish of 550–650. The principal Swindon manor more than two centuries earlier, in 1377, claimed 248 adult taxpayers, and this, after allowing for children and tax evaders, might also yield a total population of 400–50. Another eighty-eight taxpayers (perhaps representing 150 inhabitants) lived elsewhere in the parish in 1377, suggesting a total in the range 550–600. These calculations, like most historical statistics, are fraught with uncertainty, but they do offer a superficial impression of stability or stagnation. One other figure, a claim in 1627 that nine alehouses were too many for an adult population of fewer than 300, is perhaps an underestimate in order to strengthen an argument, but even if true would multiply up to a total population approaching 500, not far below our estimate.

Two further statistics bring the story down to Aubrey's old age. In 1676 a religious census returned 580 communicants in Swindon, which would suggest a total population of about 900. In 1697, the year of Aubrey's death, a list was made of the names of all Swindon's inhabitants. The manuscript was saved from burning by a Cirencester gentleman during the nineteenth century, and is now a little damaged, but it seems to yield a total of 795 names (791 and 808 are other people's computations). So we may be seeing a rise from 550–650 in 1640, to 800–900 by the end of the century, and Aubrey's testimony appears quite credible. A further modest rise occurred during the eighteenth century, as by 1801 the population had almost reached 1,200.

But before we tackle the eighteenth century, the 1697 list deserves a second glance. Not only does it list everyone's names, but it also assigns an occupation to each householder. Thomas Goddard, who had been lord of the principal manor for nearly fifty years, heads the list, followed by members of the Vilett family, owners of the clayland manor of Eastcott, and Henry Thompson, vicar since 1663. We know, incidentally, from another source that the vicar was forever running into debt, and borrowing money from Goddard. Five other families are listed as having independent means, and there were fifteen yeoman families, accounting for 7–8 per cent of the total population.

The largest group, nearly one-quarter of the total, was made up of labourers and their families, but there were also significant numbers of textile workers – weavers, tailors and drapers – and masons (most of them quarrymen, no doubt), together accounting for about one-sixth of the workforce. The list includes most of the trades – such as bakers, coopers, saddlers, shoemakers, barbers, butchers and carpenters – which we might expect to find in any small town of the period, as well as one or two more exotic specialists. There is a tobacco cutter and a 'translator' (probably a cobbler who concentrated on renovating old shoes), a combmaker and a cheesefactor.

The existence of five or six inns and an alehouse implies that, although Swindon did not lie on a major road and so could not benefit

The Goddard Arms (now Goddards Hotel) in High Street in 1900. An inn has stood on the site since the seventeenth century.

from passing trade, nevertheless the vigour of its market and quarrying industry was considerable. A survey in 1686 found that the town's inns could accommodate a total of fourteen travellers and no fewer than ninety-one horses; perhaps they were geared to catering for long-distance wagoners with their teams.

From a medieval urban village, therefore, Swindon graduated during the seventeenth century to the status of a small country town. It was a workaday place of tradesmen and labourers, and it had not yet developed the air of polite society which it exuded after 1800. It was still of less consequence than the neighbouring towns of Highworth and Wootton Bassett, and much less important than Cricklade and Marlborough. And it could still suffer put-downs. In 1731 a topographical writer sniffily remarked: 'It is so inconsiderable a place, that our histories take no notice of it'. As late as the 1790s, a directory introduced Swindon as, 'but a small place, though the houses are well built, and of stone'.

Eighteenth-century Swindon, as depicted on maps of 1763 and 1773, consisted of three principal streets, forming three sides of a square. High Street continued southwards as Lower Town and northwards as Brookwell Hill or Brock Hill (present-day Cricklade Street), a much steeper descent than now and the scene of a fatal coaching accident. The market square, opening off High Street, included in its centre a small circular building, presumably of wood, which housed the pillory and stocks, and was used by traders as a shelter. It may have been, or have replaced, the market cross referred to in 1662; it was in poor condition in 1750, and was demolished in 1793 using chains and a team of horses.

Opposite the square, along the western side of High Street to the junction with Wood Street, a number of eighteenth-century and earlier buildings have survived. The Bell Hotel claims to have been established in 1515, and other houses range in date from 1631 to the late eighteenth century. At the northern end of High Street, beyond the junction with Wood Street, is a building which was described by Sir John Betjeman as 'one of the most distinguished town houses in Wiltshire'. No. 42 Cricklade Street was built in 1729, and became the home of the Vilett family, who owned Eastcott manor. Its architecture of local stone and brick marries the two foundations on which Swindon is built, the limestone of Swindon Hill, and the clay of the vale.

Opposite: No. 42, Cricklade Street is the best piece of domestic architecture in Swindon, but its unfortunate position on a narrow, busy and noisy main road means that it is seldom fully appreciated by passers-by.

Wood Street, which runs west from High Street, is first recorded by name in 1599, and is so called on a map of 1763. The name presumably refers, like its namesake in Wootton Bassett, to the fact that it leads towards Braydon Forest. But it also had two more colloquial

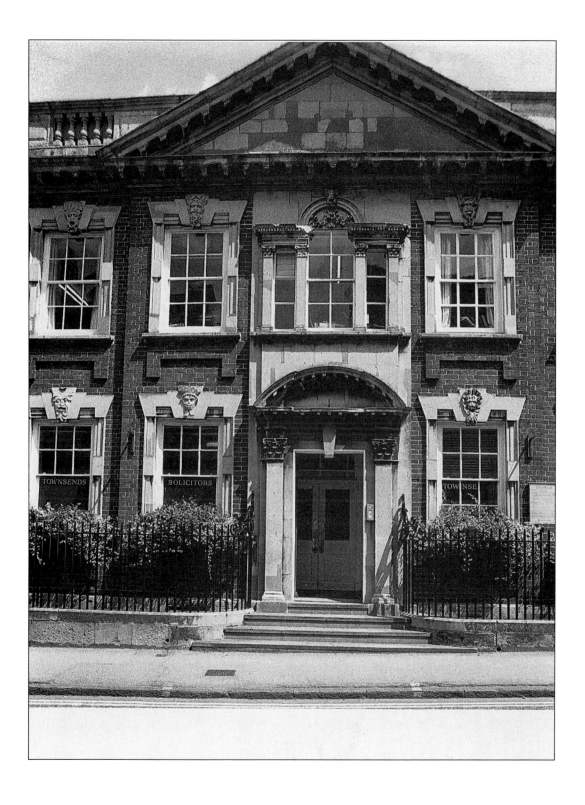

names, Blacksmith's Street and Windmill Street, both because of
premises adjoining it. It was remembered as a street of mean thatched
cottages, and this poorer quarter continued down the hill along the
lane known as Little London. Wood Street's present commercial character is largely Victorian, and results from the period when Old
Swindon traders catered also for the needs of the burgeoning new railway town.

Newport Street, the third side of the square, runs at right angles
from the southern end of High Street, and, like Wood Street, it had an
alternative name. To old men in the nineteenth century it was always
Bull Street, and was regarded as rather an eyesore. William Morris,
whom we shall encounter in the next chapter, explained its character,
and derivation from a pub, thus: 'The "Bull" was a low, thatched, cottage looking building, very much like most of the other houses on the
street. Indeed, if the houses on the street were not remarkable for their
uniformity, it was owing to their all having been put up according to
some rule of thumb. . . . In a word, the architecture of the street may
be described as that of the Squatters – of men who, by some means or
other, became possessed of a bit of land, and built themselves a house
thereon with such materials as came readiest to hand.'

Cottages in Newport Street in
about 1905.

From this description it sounds very much as if Newport Street, after the planned medieval town had failed to develop, reverted to being a country lane, and was only built up again in the seventeenth century, by informal squatting when the town's population began to grow. Short Hedge,or the Horse Fair, as the fourth side of the square of roads was known (now Devizes Road), remained in an undeveloped state until the nineteenth century.

The bases of Swindon's economy, the market and the quarries, appear to have continued throughout the eighteenth century. A regular trade by stage wagon developed with London, carrying meat, cheese and other dairy products to the capital from its depot on the site of the later town hall or corn exchange. There are dark hints too about another, clandestine, trade, in smuggled spirits brought ashore along the south coast, and concealed in the cellars of Swindon houses.

The town's character was set, and local government controlled, by its forceful leading family, the Goddards. Despite repeated disputes with the vicar over tithes, which spilled over into litigation in 1777, the Goddards were no friends of nonconformity either. Pleydell Goddard in 1741 orchestrated a savage persecution against an itinerant evangelist, John Cennick, and his followers when he tried to preach in the town. According to Cennick's diary guns, halberds and a fire engine spraying ditchwater were all turned on them to intimidate and inflict injury, while Goddard, 'sat on horseback the whole time, laughing to see us so treated'. Such anatagonism was not uncommon, but it is eloquent testimony to the power wielded by the lords of the manor that nonconformity made virtually no impact in Swindon until after 1800, even though quarrymen elsewhere were generally staunch dissenters.

This ugly episode in 1741 was still remembered when John Britton was writing eighty years later, and he contrasted such prejudice with the liberality of the Swindonians he encountered. One indication of a small measure of enlightenment dawning on the town was a free school, established in Newport Street in 1764. It was administered by a trust, and its instigator and driving force (to give him his due) was Thomas Goddard, lord of the manor. The curriculum included the three 'Rs' and religious instruction according to Anglican principles; the teaching of science and foreign languages was not permitted.

A generation later, in 1804, an Independent chapel and dissenting academy opened, also in Newport Street. Thomas and James Strange, members of a leading Swindon family of bankers and tradesmen, sponsored the venture, and the first pastor/schoolmaster was a certain George Mantell, 'a fair scholar'. But his story, and that of his nephew, Gideon Mantell, belong to the next chapter.

The First Push

Gideon Mantell spent the year 1804 in Swindon, as his uncle's pupil at the new dissenting academy in Newport Street. His home was in Sussex, but he had studied under George Mantell since 1801, and moved with him to Swindon from Westbury, where he had been an Independent pastor. George remained at Swindon until his death in 1832, building up the congregation and reputation of the Newport Street chapel, and running his school for as many as eighteen pupils at a time. Gideon stayed in Swindon little more than a year, before returning to Lewes to embark on a medical career. But it was as a geologist and palaeontologist that he made his name, and to him is

George Mantell was the first pastor of the Independent Chapel in Newport Street, which was built in 1803 and opened in 1804. It was this circumstance which brought Gideon Mantell to Swindon.

credited the discovery and first description of several dinosaur species. In later life, according to his diary, he paid four nostalgic visits to the town, in 1827, 1832, 1841 and 1846. He died in 1852.

Mantell's life spanned the most important period in Swindon's history. His schoolday memories, of reading poetry in the shade of the schoolhouse eaves, strolling in the 'Long Walk' (part of the Lawn) with his adolescent first love (who was a daughter of the prominent Strange family), and collecting in the quarries the first of the fossils which would shape his life – these were recollections of the genteel country town appreciated by John Britton. They are paralleled by the school bills of a young lady, Miss Betty Wheeler, who was being educated at Swindon between 1796 and 1800. Expenses included writing books, dancing, shoes and gloves, a servant, a trimmed bonnet, sash and umbrella, a 'filligree caddy', and various items of haberdashery, including 8s. 8d. spent on cord for her stays.

Mantell's first return visit, shortly after the former Miss Strange's death, was accomplished by stagecoach as far as Marlborough, and then by post-chaise. And his second visit, in 1832, was only a brief stop while travelling by coach from Oxford to Bristol. But in July 1841 he was able to travel down from London, purely as a day's excursion. He started at ten, he tells us, from the Great Western Railroad at Paddington, and arrived at the Swindon station at one, from where he walked through the fields to the town. He visited scenes of his youth, but spent most time at the quarries collecting specimens, and at six walked back through the fields to the railway station, accompanied by a quarryman who carried his heavy load of fossils, to catch the seven o'clock train back to London. His last nostalgic return, in 1846, was partly to meet up with his son, a young civil engineer who was working for Brunel on new railway lines in Wiltshire.

Paradoxically, it was during Mantell's idyllic year at Swindon, 1804, that the remote hilltop town took a large step closer to the outside world. Canals were an accompaniment of the industrializing Midlands and North, and came comparatively late to the South. Nevertheless the linking of London and Bristol by water had been proposed as early as the sixteenth century, and various schemes to marry the Bristol Avon and the Thames by canal were strenuously advocated by John Aubrey. One of these was planned to extend from Malmesbury on the Avon to Wootton Bassett, heading presumably for the River Ray (a tributary of the Thames) west of Swindon. But as with most of Aubrey's ingenious projects, it came to nothing.

Renewed interest during the 1790s led to the construction of two canals across north Wiltshire in order to achieve the union of Avon

Canals of southern England.

and Thames. The Kennet and Avon Canal took the southerly route, through Devizes, the Vale of Pewsey and the Kennet Valley. Branching from it, at Semington near Melksham, the Wilts and Berks Canal struck north and then east, through Dauntsey Vale to Swindon and the Vale of White Horse.

From Chaddington near Wootton Bassett to South Marston the canal took a level course across the claylands north of Swindon Hill. This stretch was the highest point, or summit, of the navigation, and construction was carried out from west to east between 1802 and 1805. A wharf was built below Swindon, and this was in use by March 1804. The canal was completed along its whole length in 1810, and immediately plans were laid to connect it to another canal, the Thames and Severn, which ran through Stroud to Lechlade. The route of the linking canal, which came to be known as the North Wilts, was decided in 1812. It left the Wilts and Berks near Eastcott and ran north to meet the Thames and Severn at Latton. After much prevarication it was completed in 1819. Finally Coate Reservoir, to the east of Swindon, was built in 1821–2 in order to overcome chronic water shortages at the canal summit.

The sluice at Coate Reservoir, drawn in 1914.

Looking back across more than fifty years of hindsight the old William Morris and the young Richard Jefferies both saw the seeds of New Swindon in the arrival of the canal. It was 'the first push', according to Jefferies; Morris went further: 'It was not only the greatest public work that had ever been undertaken in this part of the country, but the revolution it was to effect, and the impetus it was to give to trade, was simply marvellous.' More recent historians have tended to understate its importance.

At the time its effect was fourfold. First, and of greatest immediate interest to the residents of Swindon, it led to a spectacular reduction in the price of coal. Coal from the Somerset collieries (and after the North Wilts Canal was built from the Forest of Dean as well) was the main commodity carried along the canal, and local people came to rely on the cheap and plentiful supply to such an extent that, if in winter the water froze over and the barges were stopped, enterprising local farmers took waggons to the coalfield in order to make good the deficiency.

The second consequence of the canal was to stimulate the general trade of the area, by dispelling Swindon's rather aloof reputation, often repeated, as being a town which lay aside from main lines of communication. The canal opened up Swindon's agricultural hinterland, which in turn encouraged its market, and enabled it to increase its population in line with neighbouring towns and villages. Swindon's main producers of the period, however, its stone quarriers, appear not to have exploited to any great extent the possibility of cheaper and easier transport for their product which the canal offered. This may perhaps be attributable to the hostility of William Dunsford, the canal's superintendent from 1817 to 1839. Dunsford seems to have

The canal, sketched when derelict in 1914, as seen from Bridge Street. It was formally abandoned as a waterway by Act of Parliament in the same year.

had extensive business interests 'on the side', which he tried to protect from competition, including a stone-quarry at Monkton Farleigh in west Wiltshire.

But the quarriers of Swindon did benefit from the canal in another way. During its construction (and long before Dunsford's arrival) they were called upon to supply large quantities of building and paving stone. Prodigious numbers of bricks, too, were made for the canal at temporary brickyards built close to the route. All this activity helped the local economy, which was further stimulated by the spending power of the itinerant navvies employed on building the canal. William Morris sarcastically comments on local people's supposed altruism regarding the navvies' welfare, 'especially so long as they had any money to spare, not of course for the purpose of getting it from them, but only to help them to take care of it, and see that it was not lost'.

But in addition to the effects which the canal had on Swindon at the time, there are two other reasons for emphasising its importance in the town's development. The first, which we shall consider shortly, is that its presence was one of the reasons expressed in 1840 for locating the railway works at Swindon. The second is the profound effect it has had on the topography of New Swindon.

Prior to the nineteenth century, as we have seen, the boggy clay-lands north of Swindon Hill were very sparsely populated. Apart from Westcott and Eastcott Farms maps show nothing, and Britton reported that local people regarded one area, which they called 'quaving-gogs', as dangerous because of its deep quagmires. The building of the canal established a kind of base-line across the site of New Swindon which can still be clearly traced today. From the Cambria Bridge area it runs north-eastwards to become Canal Walk and the Parade, two of Swindon's principal shopping streets; then its line is followed by Fleming Way to the 'Magic Roundabout', which is close to the site of Swindon Wharf. The railway, railway village, and Victorian housing in the Manchester Road area all owe their alignment to the canal. And because it was still very much in use while New Swindon developed and grew it acted as a barrier, so that anyone wishing to cross it had to use one of five bridges. These – Cambria Bridge, Milton Road Bridge, Golden Lion Bridge, Whale Bridge and Wharf Bridge – therefore behaved as benchmarks, dictating the northern ends of Commercial Road, Regent Street and Princes Street, and therefore influencing the entire layout of the Victorian town.

But these are matters for later chapters, and must wait until we have considered the circumstances and consequences of a certain famous

Even Swindon and its surroundings, mapped in 1773.

picnic. Between 1801 and 1841 Swindon's population (excluding the recently arrived railway workers and itinerant navvies) increased by over 60 per cent, from 1,198 to 1,952. Highworth, Wroughton and Wootton Bassett all returned increases of the same order. Swindon, therefore, was developing in line with its neighbours. Their increase was rather higher than Wiltshire as a whole (40 per cent), but not quite as high as the United Kingdom average (almost 70 per cent) over the same period. As Sir John Betjeman remarked: 'Anyone wishing to see

John Street Bridge on the North Wilts. Canal. The site, close to Fleming Way and the Parade, is now completely transformed.

what Swindon would have looked like . . . [if the railway works had not come] has only to look at Highworth, once the chief town of this corner of Wiltshire.'

There were a few buildings at Swindon Wharf, including a gentleman's villa, 'surpassing the second, and approaching the first class', according to William Cobbett in 1826 – the gentleman in question was William Dunsford, the canal's entrepreneurial superintendent. But apart from the wharf, Swindon's 60 per cent growth to 1841 was absorbed within the existing town on the hill. Evidence of the prosperity and expansion of these years may still be seen at Old Town. As a schoolboy in 1804 Gideon Mantell drew a sketch map of Swindon, and this shows that Devizes Road (then known as Short Hedge or Horse Fair) was only built up at its northern end, where it joins Wood Street. Here six quarryman's houses are depicted, three on the street, three set back along a lane. By 1818 Britannia Place had begun to be developed, and by 1841 there were twelve houses in Devizes Road itself. North of Wood Street, in Little London, was an area of poor houses, including a common lodging-house, and to the west developed the fashionable quarter of the town. Here, along Bath Road (then called The Sands) was built Apsley House, which is now Swindon Museum, as well as the urbane brick terrace of town houses beyond, each with its cast-iron porch, and Prospect Place to the north, enjoying the open vista across the clay vale.

That vista was not to remain unaltered for long. In July 1833 a young engineer, Isambard Kingdom Brunel, was appointed in Bristol by a company which in the following month adopted the name 'Great Western Railway', Its aim was to link London, Bath and Bristol by rail. A route via Wootton Bassett and Wantage had been surveyed as

Opposite: Elegant town houses of about 1835 in Bath Road, Old Swindon. They represent the modest expansion of the town which was under way before the railway arrived.

Great Western and other early
railways.

early as 1824, and a similar line was recommended by Brunel in preference to the more southerly option, through the Vale of Pewsey.
Parliamentary approval for the railway was secured in August 1835,
and work began from both ends. This triggered residents of Bath's
rival, Cheltenham, to petition for a connecting line from Swindon to
Cheltenham, which was duly authorized in June 1836 as the
Cheltenham and Great Western Union Railway. In December 1840 the
railway from London reached Swindon, and a temporary station was
built at Hay Lane, between Swindon and Wootton Bassett. In May
1841 the first leg of the Cheltenham line, as far as Cirencester, was
completed, and in the following month Box Tunnel, the last and greatest obstacle on the line west to Bristol, was conquered, so that trains
could begin to run between London and Bristol. Gideon Mantell, when
he visited Swindon in July 1841 aboard the Bristol train, must therefore have been one of the first passengers. Swindon Junction Station,
although in use from about May 1841, was not completed until July
1842, and the link with Cheltenham was finished in May 1845.

It is no use trying to appreciate these bald, but momentous state-
ments, unless we are prepared to dispel from our minds our hindsight
of all that was to follow, and to put ourselves into Mantell's shoes, as
he made his way across the fields back to the station with his fossils in
1841. The railways planned and built in the 1830s were the direct
result of two factors: the success of the Liverpool and Manchester
Railway (opened in 1830) in showing that steam locomotion between

A lithograph of New Swindon in 1845, as Gideon Mantell would have seen it during his last visit to the town.

cities was a viable and profitable undertaking; and the availability of capital (and willingness of its owners) to speculate in similar projects. Of the hundred or so railway companies sanctioned by 1840 most were concerned with relatively short distances; indeed by 1844 only 2,000 miles of track had been laid. The Great Western scheme was among the most ambitious of the early schemes, and was paralleled only by the Grand Junction (Liverpool to Birmingham) and the London and Birmingham, both opened in 1838. For shareholders, directors, contractors and employees alike – let alone passengers – the enterprise was fraught with risk and uncertainty.

For the Wiltshire countryman the possibility of a railway provoked a mixture of responses. Some, like the old farmer recalled in an anecdote by William Morris, refused to countenance the existence of such a thing. On being told about it, he took the news as, 'a most wicked and deliberate attempt on the part of an old friend to deceive and mislead him,' and could not believe that there would ever be a mode of travel to surpass the yellow post chaise which he had seen with his own eyes. Others, including many landowners, greeted the prospect with hostility, regarding it as an intrusion on the privacy of their estates, and an unwelcome move towards social equality. In engineering their routes, railway companies repeatedly bent to the demands of landed interests. In Swindon the lord of the manor, Ambrose Goddard, opposed a plan to build the line to the south of the canal with a station at the foot of Drove Road because it impinged on his parkland.

But such opposition was rarely fuelled by simple prejudice or inconvenience. Goddard, for example, as well as looking after his Swindon interests, was also from 1835 chairman of the Wilts and

SWINDON, WILTS.
A FREEHOLD ESTATE,

(Bounded on the south side by the line of the " Great Western Railway," and on the west side by the line of the projected " Cheltenham and Great Western Union Railway," and the North Wilts Canal ;)

FOR Peremptory SALE by PUBLIC AUCTION, by W. DORE, (by order of Trustees), at the BELL INN, in *Swindon*, on MONDAY the 18th day of April, 1836, precisely at four o'clock in the afternoon, under conditions ; consisting of three Inclosures of very useful and productive Mea ow or Pasture LAND, containing together by admeasurement 21A. 3R. 15P., lying in the tything of Eastcott, in the parish of Swindon, and now occupied by most respectable yearly tenants.

This little Estate, independent of its locality, is desirable but when it is considered that both the above Railways will touch upon, or very near it, and that the important depot for the junction of the Cheltenham with the Great Western is not unlikely to be actually upon, and must be at all events very near this Property, its future value is incalculable. The speculator will rarely meet with such an opportunity of reaping profit at little risk. The Land Tax is redeemed, and it is divided into three Fields, and will be sold in two lots, as follows :

	A.	R.	P
Lot 1.--Loppos Hill Grounds, with useful Stalls thereon, contains	12	3	32
York's Upper Breach	6	3	16
Lot 2.--The Three Acres, formerly part of Loppos Hill	2	0	7
Total	21	3	15

Part of the Purchase Money may remain on Mortgage, if required.

For further information, apply to Messrs. CROWDY Solicitors, Swindon.

A remarkable advertisement, which appeared in the *Devizes and Wiltshire Gazette* in April 1836, several weeks before the Cheltenham branch was sanctioned, and more than four years before the decisio n was taken to build the railway works at Swindon. On the file copy of the newspaper, here reproduced, someone has unfortunately struck the advertisement through with a pen.

Berks Canal, whose fate was closely bound up with the new railway. Many local people watched the progress of the railway with interest, not as a potential threat but as a possible source of riches. In April 1836, before the Cheltenham branch was even ratified by parliament, an advertisement appeared in a Wiltshire newspaper advertising fields at Eastcott for sale. Because of their proximity to the proposed railway lines, and the likelihood that a railway depot would be built near them – if not actually on them – it was claimed that they had an 'incalculable' future value. As it turned out, of course, the advertisement was no exaggeration, and Richard Jefferies recalled that one or two fortunes were made out of land which hitherto had been scarcely worth the trouble of attending to, and covered with furze.

If the prospect of becoming a railway junction was greeted with a mixture of prejudice, uncertainty and excited speculation, it was overshadowed in 1840 by an even more far-reaching proposal. Daniel Gooch, an ambitious engineer from Northumberland, was twenty years old when appointed Brunel's superintendent of locomotives in 1837. By 1840, with engines in service over much of the line and the prospect of completion to Bristol within months, Gooch was asked to recommend a site for a locomotive repair depot. His choice was Swindon, and in a letter to Brunel on 13 September he set out some of his reasons.

Part of Swindon's tithe map, drawn in about 1840, which shows the relationship of the canals, the new railways, and the existing field boundaries which were soon to be overrun by houses and the railway works.

Locomotives of the period were not considered capable of operating the entire distance from London to Bristol, and so a change would be necessary. Although Swindon was not halfway, it did lie at the transition from relatively flat and easy going up the Thames Valley to the shorter but more demanding descent through Box to Bath and Bristol. Swindon would be the convenient point at which to change to and from more powerful engines to tackle the western section. Furthermore, some kind of premises would in any case be necessary at Swindon, both to accommodate banking and pilot engines, and as a station to serve the junction with the Cheltenham line. Centralizing repairs there as well would be a sensible economy.

Gooch noted also that a suitable, level site was available in the angle formed by the junction of the two lines, and that the canal existed nearby, which would enable coal at a reasonable price to be brought to the depot. The principal drawback of Swindon, in Gooch's mind, was a poor water supply, but that in the last resort might be remedied by using the canal.

Soon after receiving the letter Gooch and Brunel visited the site, taking their lunch with them. The reality of the lunch is attested by Gooch's diary, and the story of the picnic, 'on the greensward which was then where the platform is now', was described in picturesque detail (including blossoming furze and frisking rabbits) by Richard Jefferies in an essay about Swindon published in 1875. Jefferies apparently was not aware of it when he wrote an earlier account of Swindon's origins in 1867, and in 1875 he wrongly attributes it to determining the line of the railway – this of course had been done much earlier, before Gooch worked for the Great Western. By 1913 the picnic legend ended with a stone, or even a sandwich, being thrown to decide upon the actual site of the railway works. Wittingly or unwittingly the foundation of plebeian New Swindon thereby paralleled that of its Wiltshire rival, patrician New Salisbury, whose site had been chosen (according to one version of the legend) by the flight of an arrow, shot by the bishop from the ramparts of Old Sarum Castle.

Irrespective of the existence of any primeval railway sandwich, Brunel agreed with Gooch about his choice of Swindon, and the decision was endorsed by the Great Western Railway board of directors on 6th October. But the apparently cogent operational reasons for the decision advanced by Gooch are by no means the whole story. Several recent authors have pointed out the impracticabilities of the scheme. In the first place the problem of water supply had not been adequately resolved. In fact poor water and sanitation were to blight the railway

A portrait of Sir Daniel Gooch published in 1868.

second place there was no obvious reason why the repair works should be cited alongside a depot for operational locomotives, especially on what was in effect a virgin site with no pool of skilled labour available. In the third place, whilst it was true that the canal at Swindon offered a cheap coal supply from areas not at the time accessible by railway, the same could be argued about Bristol, Bath or Chippenham, which were all much closer to the Somerset coalfield. Would not Bristol, where labour, water, housing and coal were all obtainable, have made better sense?

To explain Gooch's preference for Swindon there have been suggestions that he was in some sense implicated in land deals, or was being offered a commission on profits by speculators; and it has been observed that by 1852 he was able to spend £13,400 (a considerable fortune at Victorian prices) on buying Nythe Farm near Wanborough. Clearly he could have had financial interests in developing Swindon which he never declared, and it would be naive to think that no private consultations ever took place between Gooch and prominent Swindonians. It would be particularly interesting, for example, to know whether any deals were done with the Wilts and Berks Canal, and its chairman, Ambrose Goddard, which were not revealed to the respective companies' directors.

But there is probably no need to tarnish the reputation of Daniel Gooch in order to explain his advocacy of Swindon. Britain between 1837 and 1842 was in severe recession, and this not only applied the brakes to new railway schemes, but also forced companies which were already committed to building lines to seek economies wherever possible. The Great Western was in particular difficulty since building costs had far outstripped estimates. Now the site at Swindon for the locomotive repair works recommended by Gooch already belonged to a railway company, the Cheltenham and Great Western Union. It is not known how or why the company acquired it, but it was a valuable asset, since transferring it to the Great Western enabled the smaller company to extract certain operating concessions from the larger, and the larger to acquire the site for its works with virtually no expenditure at all.

The next problem which the impoverished Great Western board had to face was the cost of building workers' housing and an appropriate station complex for the railway junction. Gooch's plan offered the solution. He had made out a persuasive case for Swindon as the point at which engines should be changed. The resulting delay to the train could best be occupied and disguised by providing passengers with refreshments. Such a concept was of course perfectly familiar to travellers brought up on stagecoaches, and it was already practised at Wolverton, the equivalent point on the London and Birmingham Railway. By February 1841, four months after Gooch's recommendation had been approved, the company was ready to announce that it had made a deal whereby a construction firm built the station and the railway village at its own expense, in return for the exclusive franchise of the refreshment facility, and the rents of the workers' cottages. By choosing Swindon, therefore, the company obtained its station, its workers' housing and the site of its works for nothing.

Gideon Mantell paid a last visit to Swindon in 1846. By then the station, the works and much of the railway village had been built. But 1846 was another important year in Swindon's evolution. The works, as we have seen, were designed for the repair of existing locomotives. In 1846, for the first time, new locomotives were manufactured at the works, and Swindon's revolution was fulfilled.

The view from the gallery or footbridge at Swindon Station, published in an 1852 guidebook. Notice the broad gauge track and locomotive.

CHAPTER FOUR

A God of Steam

L ike Crewe, Swindon during the 1840s rose from obscurity to become a household name. 'Swindon, all-important Swindon,' boasted a promotional guidebook to the Great Western Railway in 1852; 'who that knows aught of railways, or railway travelling, has not heard of Swindon's world-wide reputation, as well for the vastness of its workshops and engine depot, as for the admirable and splendid accommodation that it furnishes to the way-worn traveller?' A page of mouthwatering grandiloquence follows about the station refreshment rooms, ending with the opinion that, 'here we have a close approximation to

An idealized portrayal of the refreshment rooms for first-class passengers at Swindon Station in 1852.

perfection, accompanied, too, with undeviating civility, and a moderate tariff'.

The guidebook writer, replete no doubt with free helpings of the banbury-cakes and sherry-cobler which he eulogized, was probably correct in his opinion that Swindon's reputation was made on its refreshment rooms. But it was not the reputation that it might have wished. Others did not share his enthusiasm, either about the quality or price of the 'choice refections'; indeed the nickname 'Swindleum' began to be applied to the establishment. Brunel himself was among the first to complain, within months of its opening. His letter to the caterer has often been quoted, in which he denies calling the coffee 'inferior' – he had actually called it 'bad roasted corn'. Unfortunately for Swindon, it was the enforced refreshment stop and the exorbitant prices which travellers first encountered, and which stuck in their memories, rather than the other themes with which the present chapter is concerned: the locomotive works, the railway village, and the effect of the new town on the old. So we had better dispose of this embarrassing topic first.

Swindon Junction Station, with its elaborate refreshment rooms and hotel, was built in 1841–2 by J. & C. Rigby, a London firm of builders and civil engineers, at their own expense, and its architecture survived largely unscathed until redevelopment of the site began in July 1972. The buildings comprised two three-story blocks with basements, linked by a footbridge which straddled the main line. The ornate refreshment rooms, for first and second class passengers (segregated) only, were at ground floor level, with kitchens below and hotel above.

The station buildings at Swindon depicted in George Measom's 1852 guide to the Great Western Railway. Later editions of the guidebook tended to gloss over Swindon.

As part of the deal Messrs. Rigby were leased the sole catering franchise at Swindon for ninety-nine years on a peppercorn rent. In the early days a change of engine at Swindon was an operational necessity, as we have seen, and so the company agreed that all trains would make a refreshment stop of about ten minutes at Swindon. Rigbys sublet and eventually sold this franchise, but the ten-minute stop was rigorously enforced by the caterer long after the change of engine was no longer necessary. This exasperating delay, along with the exorbitant prices charged for mediocre food, continued to irritate the company and its passengers until 1895, when the GWR paid the princely sum of £100,000 to buy out the franchise-holder. By then, of course, the Swindon refreshment rooms, and by association the town itself, had become the butt of music-hall humour.

The locomotive depot and repair works, sanctioned by the board in October 1840, were begun in 1841 and completed before the end of 1842, for regular use from January 1843. Brunel was responsible for designing them to Gooch's requirements (the job was probably delegated to an assistant, T.H. Bertram), and J. & C. Rigby were employed as contractors. At the heart of the original works were two large sheds, abutting to form a T-shape. The cross-piece of the T, parallel with the Bristol line to its south, was the engine shed; adjoining it on its northern side was the repair shop. Other necessary buildings, including the smiths' shops, wagon shops, the erecting shop and the offices, were arranged around this T, rather like quadrangles around an Oxford college. The master of the establishment, under Daniel Gooch, was a Scotsman, Archibald Sturrock. Like Gooch he was in his early twenties, and the two men had become friends before either joined the GWR. He stayed with the company, as works superintendent, until 1850, then was employed for sixteen years by the Great Northern Railway. In 1866, aged fifty, he retired, but did not die until New Year's Day 1909, forty-two years later.

The works quickly progressed from repairing to manufacturing rolling stock, including carriages and wagons, and in February 1846 the first locomotive, named *Premier*, was produced. The GWR, locked in controversy over the merits of the broad gauge compared with its rivals' narrow (now standard) gauge, was eager to show its superiority, and in January 1846 Gooch was instructed to build, 'a colossal locomotive working with all speed'. Thirteen weeks later the engine, *Great Western*, was running, and showed that it was capable of hauling passenger trains over long distances at an average speed of nearly 60 m.p.h. Twenty-eight more express passenger locomotives were built at Swindon between 1846 and 1851, as well as many smaller

'The Lord of the Isles', a famous product of the Swindon workshops. which was displayed at the 1851 Crystal Palace exhibition. It stands outside the railway church, St Mark's.

Opposite: (above) Plan of the railway works in 1846. Notice that the railway village is only partially built, and that the boundaries of the new development correspond with those of the fields shown on the tithe map of about 1840 (p. 62); (below) Part of the panorama of New Swindon painted by Edward Snell in 1849, showing the railway works. The painting, now in Swindon Railway Museum, is remarkable for its detail, such as the stagecoach being hauled by the train arriving on the Cheltenham line in the background. The rest of the panorama is reproduced on p. 50.

goods engines. They established the works at the forefront of railway technology, and its reputation was underscored in 1851 when one of its progeny, *Lord of the Isles*, was exhibited at the Great Exhibition.

But reputation was not enough. Swindon began its manufacturing career during the railway mania of 1844–7, when companies such as the GWR over-reached themselves with ambitious plans for expansion. Following the repeal of the Corn Laws in 1846 and the influx of cheap imported grain the stock market collapsed in 1847. The GWR was in serious financial trouble and retrenched its operations. At Swindon the workforce had risen from about 400 in 1843 to 1,800 by 1847, after which it was savagely cut to 600. Several senior officers, including Sturrock, resigned rather than face a cut in salary. Recovery was gradual, but at Swindon it was helped by a new dimension during the 1850s, as the GWR acquired Midland companies operating narrow (standard) gauge lines, and required locomotives and rolling stock for them.

Railway engineering in general, and Swindon works in particular, was the high technology of the 1840s; it demanded a workforce quite different from either the uncouth navvies who built the lines, or the pastoral farmhands who inhabited the neighbouring north Wiltshire countryside. Skilled engineers and fabricators, like oilfield workers

The engine house in 1846, where routine maintenance to locomotives was carried out. The house could accommodate thirty-six engines, like horses in stables (an unconscious echo of the stagecoach era?). A mobile platform travelled along the house, to enable the engines to be moved from stall to stall.

in the North Sea during the 1980s, commanded a high premium, and travelled to Swindon from all over the country to work hard for high wages. Analysis of the 1851 census for New Swindon shows that nearly 15 per cent of the population originated in Scotland or Northern England, and nearly 10 per cent in London and the south-east; the equivalent proportions in Old Swindon were 1 per cent and 4 per cent. A recent study has identified the careers of many New Swindon pioneers, and shows that some were 'headhunted' by Gooch and Sturrock from places where they had worked previously – Dundee, the north-east and south Lancashire. There seems even to have been a kind of recruitment agency operating for Gooch in Liverpool.

It was clear to the GWR board when they decided to site the works at Swindon that accommodation for their employees would have to be provided. We have already described the deal whereby J. & C. Rigby built at their own expense cottages for the workforce on land which the GWR had purchased, in return for fixed rents from the occupants. It is time now to examine the outcome of this arrangement.

The development of New Swindon as a community may be compared with two other English towns which owed their origins to railway works on 'green field' sites, Crewe in Cheshire, and Wolverton in Buckinghamshire, now part of Milton Keynes. Wolverton's railway works were begun by the London and Birmingham Railway in 1838 and, like Swindon, were sited at the point on the line where a change of engine was necessary. The population grew from 417 in 1831 to 2,070 in 1851, and the new town was built as a grid of 242 red-brick terraced houses, with a church, a school and several pubs. That Wolverton was in the GWR directors' minds when they sanctioned the development at Swindon is clear from their report, in which the place is specifically mentioned. Crewe, the creation of the Grand Junction Railway, was exactly contemporary with Swindon, since its railway works were begun in 1841. Early housing, some with Gothic detailing, included a range of accommodation reflecting the status of its occupants within the works.

At Swindon two blocks of four parallel streets were laid out and built up with terraces of cottages, largely between 1842 and 1846. The streets took their names from destinations of the trains which passed

Restored cottages in the railway village.

nearby – Bristol, Bath, Exeter and Taunton comprised the western block, London, Oxford, Reading and Faringdon the eastern block. The western block was built up quickly, mostly in 1842 and 1843, but the eastern block took much longer to complete. The terraces are of two-storey cottages, generally with one or two bedrooms, and built of oolitic limestone extracted during the building of Box Tunnel. Between the two blocks of terraces, running north towards the works entrance, was a wide boulevard-like area originally called High Street, and by 1848 larger houses had been erected facing it at the end of each terrace. The Mechanics' Institution and Medical Fund Hospital were subsequently built on this open area, and it was renamed Emlyn Square after Viscount Emlyn, a GWR chairman. Most of the railway village, as this estate is known, was purchased by the local authority in 1966, and renovated between 1969 and 1980. One cottage (which is, however, not typical of the estate as a whole, since it is later and larger than most) was opened as a museum in 1980, and has been furnished and decorated to appear as it might have done in about 1900.

Since 1945, and perhaps before, a tradition has grown up in Swindon that the railway village was designed by the eminent Victorian architect and architectural writer, Sir Matthew Digby Wyatt. It is true that between 1852 and 1854 he collaborated with Brunel on the design of Paddington Station, and so had a connection with the GWR. But that was later. In 1841, when work began on the railway village, he was barely twenty, and was saving to go on the Grand Tour by working in a drawing office, and also undertaking small architectural commissions – a school in Wales, two houses near Dublin and a London factory building. While it is possible that Messrs. Rigby sought his help for Swindon, no connection with the project is mentioned by his biographers or appears in his list of works. Another objection to the theory of his involvement is that, although the railway village has a unified appearance, there are significant differences of architectural detail between the terraces, as if modifications were made as the building work progressed. Wyatt spent two years, 1844–6, touring on the continent, and so could not have been directly involved with the project as it took shape.

The railway village repays study nevertheless. The problem of housing large working communities close to new industrial complexes was not new in the 1840s. It had been faced by colliery and mill owners in the Midlands and North for several decades, as the industrial revolution invaded remote and unpopulated areas. Some of the resulting employer housing was of very poor quality, but by the 1830s two arguments had emerged for providing reasonably good living conditions for the workforce – that they helped to recruit suitable and desirable employees, and that they enhanced productivity by reducing illness and improving morale. What had not yet emerged by 1840 were the conclusions of inquiries linking poor sanitation and water supply with disease, which led to the passing of public health legislation in 1848. Nor was the era of philanthropic housing schemes, initiated by benevolent societies and conscientious employers, yet under way, although it was just beginning, and a few notable experiments had been tried.

It was against this background that the railway village emerged. Despite the aura of paternalism which the company later managed to convey, the GWR in the 1840s was not, and could not afford to be, a philanthropic organization. It could not justify to its shareholders what might be seen as unnecessary expenditure on moral or religious grounds. In fact it rather side-stepped responsibility for housing its workers through its deal with J. & C. Rigby. And Rigbys, driven no doubt by normal commercial considerations of the rate of return on their investment, built to a standard which they considered would warrant the rent which skilled engineering workers could be expected to pay. If that standard was quite high, it was because Rigbys had saved money by not having had to purchase the site, there was a bountiful supply of good building stone, and the intended occupants were comparatively well paid. The main drawback, which was exacerbated by early overcrowding in the village, was the old bugbear which Gooch had identified in his original report, the problem of water supply and drainage.

Edward Snell, who became Assistant Works Manager in about 1849, and who painted the famous panorama of New Swindon in that year, was one of the first inhabitants of the railway village, arriving at the end of February 1843. Soon afterwards he wrote in his diary: 'For my part I hate it and haven't been well since I've been here. . . . A precious place it is at present, not a knocker or a scraper in the whole place. Most of the houses very damp and containing only two rooms. . . . Not a drop of water to be had but what comes from the tenders or out of ditches and what little we do get is as thick as mud – not fit for a jackass to drink. The Company make the men pay most extortionate rents for these bits of huts, too – 3s. 6d. for a single and 7s. for a double cottage and won't allow any of the men in their employ to sell anything whatever. We have a couple of Doctors' Shops which are pretty frequently visited, a Great Western Sick Club, a school . . . and a chapel.'

Snell's experience confirms the impression of squalid, overcrowded and unhealthy conditions given by other sources, although it may have seemed worse to him – he was born in Barnstaple and apprenticed in Bath – than to other newcomers accustomed to Sunderland or Liverpool. His mention of the various social amenities already available in New Swindon is remarkable, because, written in 1843, it antedates the usually accepted date for any of them. He cannot have made them up, however, and the existence of the chapel is confirmed by a document preserved at Gloucester. This records that in June 1843 a group of Methodists were holding services in a room next to the Golden Lion Inn near the Swindon Railroad Station; they were under the leadership of a Wesleyan minister from Marlborough with a wonderfully Old Testament name, Zephaniah Job.

During the 1840s and 1850s the amenities mentioned by Snell, and several others, became established in their own buildings. They were supported by the company in various ways, and some acquired GWR as a handle to their names, but in general they did not originate with the company and were not officially funded. Thus the GWR church (St Mark's) and the GWR school next to it resulted from a bequest in

Another part of Edward Snell's 1849 panorama of New Swindon (see p. 44). The regularity of the railway village, and the open area at its centre, are clearly seen, as well as St Mark's Church in the foreground.

An engraving of St Mark's Church which was published in the *Illustrated London News* to accompany an account of its opening.

1842 by C.H. Gibbs, a director, and were built on land donated by Colonel Vilett. St Mark's Church, 'all spikes and prickles outside', was completed in 1845 on land immediately west of the railway village. In an essay published in 1952 Sir John Betjeman paid the church, and the community which worshipped there, a unique compliment: 'One cannot call it a convenient site. . . . But it is a strong church and though it is not much to look at, it is for me the most loved church in England.' The school opened during the same year, and was soon suffering the same overcrowding as the rest of the village. In 1847 it had 168 pupils and only two teachers. The GWR park, abutting the school and church, was given by Colonel Vilett to the company as a public amenity in 1844.

The two most prestigious organizations stemming from the early years of the railway village were the mechanics' institute and the medical fund. Gooch claimed to have started the institute in January 1844, in response to complaints from the neighbouring gentry about drunkenness and disorder: 'I got together those of the workmen whose moral character was superior to their fellows and formed them into a Workmen's Institute.' In fact its genesis probably lay in an informal lending library begun by employees a few months' earlier. Under the name 'New Swindon Mechanics' Institution' the organization rapidly grew, and provided not only evening classes and the library, but also entertainments of various kinds, including theatre, concerts and dances. One event organized by the institute in 1849, a free excursion to Oxford, proved so successful that an annual 'Trip' by train developed as a kind of works' outing, and ultimately as the annual holiday for employees and their families. In 1855 the mechanics' institute moved into purpose-built premises in the centre of the railway village, which had been built by a company set up for the purpose and chaired by the works superintendent. An octagonal market hall adjoined the institute building.

The GWR Medical Fund Society traced its origins to the period of distress caused by the lay-offs and short-time working introduced in 1847. It appears to have been an employee-led initiative to create a fund which would pay the surgeon to attend both working and laid-off staff and their families. To pay for the scheme every employed man would pay a small weekly subscription, but Gooch successfully sought company blessing, and assistance in the form of a rent-free house in the railway village for the surgeon, and an annual stipend for the surgeon to cover attendance to accidents at work. A society was formed to administer the fund, and this eventually grew to such proportions that in 1871 it built and administered its own hospital next to the mechanics' institute.

The unpopular 'Barracks', or hostel for single men in the railway village. At the time of this drawing, in 1914, it was in use as a Wesleyan chapel; now it houses Swindon's GWR museum.

Opposite: (above) The reading room within the Mechanics' Institute, sketched in 1914; (below) waiting for the start of the GWR 'Trip' in 1910. Two products of the Swindon works, *County of Monmouth* and *County of Somerset*, prepare to haul their makers and families to the seaside.

One other prominent establishment of the period was intended to solve the overcrowding problem. This was a lodging-house for single men, which Richard Jefferies claimed could accommodate 500, and was 'a vast place, with innumerable rooms and corridors'. It was begun in 1849 and completed in 1852, but the austere pile was immediately unpopular, and was nicknamed the 'Barracks'. Little occupied, it was later turned into flats for an influx of Welsh workers, then sold to become a chapel, and since 1962 has been the railway museum.

In 1850, and for many years to come, there was open countryside stretching down the hillside which separated old, respectable Swindon from this alien aberration of the railway revolution. How strange, how disconcerting, how fascinating it all must have seemed to the Wiltshire countryman – the unintelligible accents of the newcomers, the fearsome power unleashed by the engines, the massive buildings, spanking new. That intervening mile of grass and agriculture was doubtless a comfort to many in Old Swindon, but it was not far enough to allow the town to vegetate in some xenophobic cocoon. In fact the effect on it of New Swindon was profound. A government inspector, called in to examine the town's public health, reported in 1850 that: 'The old town of Swindon has materially increased in numbers and wealth since the completion of the railway. The houses built have been of a superior class; and the tenants, being more or less connected with the railway, are a well-behaved and intelligent class of persons.'

So this was one consequence of the railway works, that some of the better-paid employees found their way up the hill and made their homes in Old Swindon. But many more of the newcomers, wives and young children especially, were familiar with the trek across the fields for another reason. In the early years of the railway village there were few shops, and most food and provisions consumed in New Swindon had been purchased in the old town, and carried back down Eastcott Hill, which was then a narrow field path. 'Those were rosy days for Old Swindon shopkeepers and publicans', recalled an old man who had grown up at Prospect in the 1860s. The railway workers were paid fortnightly, on alternate Fridays, and then large sums of money changed hands in Old Town.

There is no doubt that wealth created in the railway works stimulat-ed Old Swindon's economy. But even without that the town seems to have been doing well during the 1840s. A directory description pub-lished in 1848 was particularly up-beat about Swindon's progress. New streets were being laid out, the general appearance of the town was improving, and the shops now equalled those of Bath and Cheltenham. A large assembly room had recently been added to the Goddard Arms, and there were plans to build a town hall and market house. The old church was too small for the growing population, and so there were proposals to replace it with a new one. The cattle market was making a great name for itself, and the flourishing quarries were major employers. All in all, 'Swindon may now, perhaps, be said to be one of the most flourishing and promising towns in Wiltshire'.

The permanent (as opposed to transient) population of Old Swindon in 1841 cannot be accurately deduced from the census, but was proba-bly of the order of 1,800 to 1,850. In 1851 it was 2,294, which repre-sented a rise of about 25 per cent. To accommodate the extra families new houses were built and new streets laid out. They were given patri-otic names – Britannia Place, Victoria Street, Albert Street, Union Row – and most of them have survived to the present day. But for all its pretensions the expanding town had problems. Sanitation was poor, water sources were becoming polluted, and disease was rife. The inspector called in to report in 1850 discovered that life expectancy

Opposite: The Italianate tower of Old Swindon's corn exchange was built in 1864 using Swindon and Bath stone. The adjoining classical town hall was built in 1852 as a covered market, but never so used. Instead the corn exchange fulfilled this purpose until the early twentieth century.

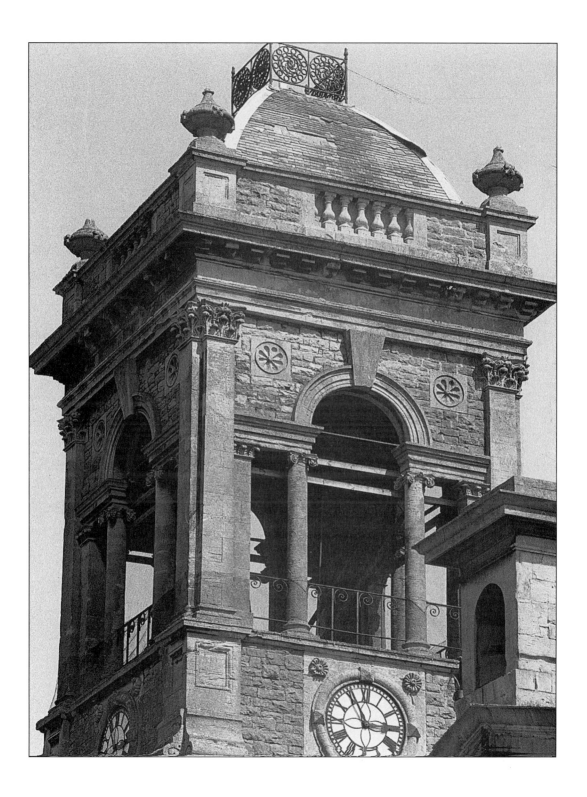

had reduced from over thirty-six years in the whole parish during the 1820s to twenty-nine years in Old Town in the 1840s. He recommended that a sewerage and water supply system be provided for the town, and that a local board be set up to oversee it.

However different Old and New Swindon might have appeared, they could not for long escape the fundamental problem common to them both – that the provision of services was not keeping pace with the rising population. These and other growing pains were to continue for another fifty years, until Old and New disappeared, and Swindon became simply Swindon again.

Brick-Built Breeding Boxes

S windon in 1851 had a population of 4,879, almost equally divided between the old and new towns. A half-century later, in 1901, the census returned a total of 45,006, and no longer distinguished between old and new. This was because in the previous year the two communities had united to become a municipal borough. During the same half-century the population of England and Wales rose by 81 per cent; but that of Wiltshire rose by only 8 per cent, and if Swindon is left out of the reckoning, the rest of Wiltshire's population actually declined by 8 per cent. Swindon meanwhile increased by nothing short of 822 per cent. The purpose of the present chapter is to account for this astounding statistic, and to examine its impact on the Swindon which we see around us.

We left the railway works in trouble at the end of the 1840s, with its workforce slashed to 600. By 1900 the payroll had risen by leaps and bounds to about 11,500. Four interrelated factors were responsible not only for the leaps and bounds, but also for intervening episodes of set-back and disappointment. First were periods of expansion and retrenchment in the national economy of Victorian England. Second were technical improvements and new legislation affecting railways. Third were the fortunes of the Great Western Railway, as it built new lines and took over competitors, but also teetered towards bankruptcy. And fourth were decisions taken by the company's directors to centralize its engineering activities at Swindon.

Recovery after the desperate days of 1847–9 was accomplished at first by diversifying to build components for bridges and other civil engineering works. Later, in 1854, the GWR purchased rival companies in the Midlands which used the narrow, or standard, gauge. This resulted in the need for new locomotives and rolling stock, which Swindon began to produce in 1855. Then in 1860–1 Daniel Gooch persuaded his board to build a rolling mill at the works, which would produce better and cheaper iron rails than they could obtain from outside contractors, and would also be a way of recycling scrap iron from Swindon's other manufacturing processes. During another railway boom in the 1860s the GWR, saddled with its broad gauge, was beleagured by competing railways who tried to encroach on its territory with plans for standard gauge lines, and large sums were spent on legal actions opposing them, as well as in proposing new lines of its own. In 1866 the company had overreached itself and was almost bankrupt; it was only through skilful negotiation with its creditors that Daniel Gooch, newly appointed chairman, drew the GWR back from the abyss.

This cloud of financial ruin had a silver lining for Swindon. The company had since 1865 been thinking about establishing new carriage works at Oxford. Gooch now persuaded his board that Swindon would be a cheaper alternative, because company-owned land was already available, in the area between the railway village and the main Bristol line. Here, abutting Bristol Street and London Street, the carriage works were begun in 1868, and it is their fortress-like facade of stone and glass, some 350 m long, which for over a century separated living Swindon from working Swindon. A decade of expansion and

Railway works employees and others near the 'tunnel', or main entrance to the works, in 1912. The grim wall of the carriage works forms the backcloth.

prosperity for Swindon works followed, stimulated largely by the gradual changeover from broad to standard gauge. Orders for new locomotives and rolling stock to meet the change kept Swindon busy, and justified wholesale modernization of the factory.

The boom ended in 1877/8, and no further expansion took place at the works until 1887. Nationally these were years of severe depression, and one consequence was a reduction in demand for rail traffic. The GWR found itself over-resourced, and imposed a freeze on orders for new stock. Swindon suffered less than some other establishments, however, as the company chose to centralize work on its largest plant, and by judicious accounting, routine repairs, and work on new safety modifications, the railway works managed to tick over. This difficult period came to a sudden end in 1887, with new orders, the implementation of new safety requirements, and the run-up to the final conversion from broad to standard gauge in 1892. As the national recession drew to a close in the mid-1890s the GWR was poised to set new standards of comfort and sophistication, with improved locomotive and carriage design, and an assured future for Swindon at the head of railway technology.

Clearly, in charting the progress of the railway works to the dawn of the new century, when it employed over 11,500 (most of them male breadwinners), we have accounted for much of Swindon's spectacular rise in population. A few years later, in 1908, it was estimated that nearly 80 per cent of Swindon's male workforce were employed by the GWR. So many men inside the works left a pool of employable wives and daughters outside, and this attracted clothing factories to Swindon. The largest, Compton's in Sheppard Street, had 1,000 employees in the 1890s, and very appropriately its work included the manufacture of GWR uniforms. Even so, relatively few Swindon women (7.2 per cent in 1908) were in paid employment.

What about the men who did not work 'inside' (as employment in the railway works was always referred to), or elsewhere on the railway system? Some at Old Town were quarrymen, or were connected with the agriculture of the surrounding area. Many more worked in the various retail and service industries which the growing town required. A particular need, of course, was for houses to accommodate the multitude of newcomers, and an army of building workers moved in. They were the true creators of Victorian Swindon, and it is their legacy that we see today.

Sir John Betjeman was commissioned to write a study of architecture in Swindon to commemorate the borough's half-century in 1950. From the beautifully polished essay which resulted we may gather that

Betjeman's 'red brick rash'.
The prospect of Swindon from
Deacon Street in 1914.

he found the town interesting, but unattractive. He drew a clear distinction between architecture, of which he discovered few examples
and little to admire, and building, of which he found a great deal, and
much to criticize. But in his 1950 work he could not be too rude about
his paymasters' town. In another essay published in 1952 he was more
blunt: 'For there is no doubt that Swindon *is* superficially ugly. That
pretty model village of the eighteen-forties has developed a red brick
rash which stretches up the hill to Old Swindon and strangles it.'

The 'red brick rash' is entirely the result of piecemeal and usually
small-scale development by builders and speculators, who responded
to the housing demands of the new population, and who, in the
absence of any local government planning policy, were constrained
only by market forces and the availability of land. A good example of
this process at work is described in the autobiography of an influential
educationalist, F.H. Spencer, who was born in 1870 in a house adjoining what is now Regent Circus. Spencer recalls a character whom he
called 'Old Charlie', a tallish, thin Yorkshireman, who had made
money as a skilled mechanic at the works, and who had invested it
during the 1850s in buying Upper Eastcott farmhouse and six small
stone cottages that went with it. On to these he built a terrace of six
brick houses and a small shop, which he let out to tenants. Spencer's
parents lived in one of these houses for about thirty years, and he

F.H. Spencer in retirement. The portrait of a notable Swindonian which accompanied his autobiography published in 1938.

remembered as a teenager helping Old Charlie to work out the charges necessary to make a minimum of 7.5 per cent on a gross outlay in cottage property.

Charlie the Yorkshireman, who was 'no worse than the others' according to Spencer, called his terrace 'York Place'. Other speculators attained a kind of immortality for themselves and their families by enshrining them in street names. John Henry Harding Sheppard was a brewer in old town who owned land near the railway station and at

Kingshill. Four streets between the railway village and the station divided up his name between them during the 1870s, and following his retirement to Kent we find a field at Kingshill being built up as Ashford, Folkestone, Hythe, Kent and Maidstone Roads. George Whitehead, as well as property speculator and builder, had careers as a shopkeeper, musician and publican. His wife Beatrice, his daughter Florence, and the composer after whom his shop was named, Handel, all have adjoining streets to themselves in Gorse Hill, but his own

These two maps, separated by about forty years, show the process of urban development on a greenfield site, which was a commonplace of Victorian Britian. The earlier (above) is an extract from the tithe map of about 1840, the later (left) a large-scale Ordnance Survey plan of the 1880s. F.H. Spencer describes how Upper Eastcott Farm was bought by a small speculator and developed with housing. Regent Circus and Theatre Square now occupy the site. Notice how property boundaries shown to the west of the farmhouse on the tithe map are reflected in the development of the Commercial Road area (p. 68).

street, Whitehead Street, lies on the other side of the tracks, at least a ten-minute walk away.

Examples such as these could be multiplied from all over Victorian and Edwardian Swindon. For instance, the partners of an Old Town firm of solicitors, Messrs Butterworth, Rose, and Morrison, each have a street for their surnames, and George Montagu Butterworth and Sydney Bruce Morrison have both immortalized their middle names as well. More curiously, Edmund Jones built Maxwell Street, and James Maxwell built Edmund Street. Many other road names took their cue from the patriotic fervour of the later nineteenth century, or from national or GWR dignitaries. A few stem from allegiance to the builder's native place. Maxwell's firm came from Manchester (hence Manchester Road), and Linslade Street was named by a native of the Bedfordshire town. There were also two small neighbourhoods with Oxford overtones – Carfax, Merton, Oriel and Turl Streets; and Cobden, Harcourt and Iffley Roads – which were both the work of the Oxford Building Society and its successors.

The building societies at work on a restricted site near the railway station. During the 1870s new building around Swindon was constrained by legal difficulties over the ownership of the Vilett estate, and consequently prime building sites remained inviolate under grass until 1885.

'The people who planned these streets,' mused J.B. Priestley in disdain, as he explored Swindon on a dreary evening fifty years later, 'must have been thinking and dreaming hard about the next world, not this one: it is the only charitable conclusion.' But the reality was that they did very little planning, most (but not all) of them lived elsewhere, and, like Old Charlie, they were thinking and dreaming mainly about their 7.5 per cent return. They bid for individual plots of land or whole fields as they came on to the market, and either developed them immediately, if the works were booming and houses were in demand, or let them lie fallow for a few years, if economic conditions were less good. From sale catalogues, maps, directories and building byelaw records it is possible to trace their activities in great detail, but for present purposes a summary will suffice.

During the 1840s the railway village was the main area of growth, but speculative housing was already beginning to appear in the area of Westcott Place, following the line of a much older track known as the 'Fleet' or 'Fleetway'. And because railway works construction stimulated a temporary burst of activity at the canal wharf, a beerhouse and

Golden Lion bridge, where Bridge Street crossed the canal to become Regent Street. The first crossing, a wooden swing bridge, was replaced by this structure in 1870, and the footbridge was added in 1877. They survived until 1918. The bridge took its name from the nearby Golden Lion Inn, and a replica of the original lion now stands close to the original site, which has become the main crossroads of the pedestrianized shopping centre (see p. 104).

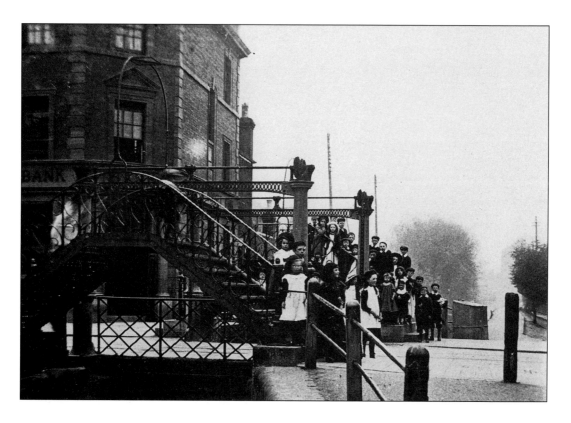

terrace of houses were built nearby. The beerhouse took its name, 'The Whale,' from the shape of the canal bridge next to it, and the houses, 'Cetus Buildings', took their rather pretentious name from the beerhouse (*cetus* is Latin for a whale). A second place of refreshment, the Golden Lion Inn, was in business by 1843, and this became a pivotal landmark in the development of the town's street plan. It stood beside the canal next to a swing-bridge, the Golden Lion Bridge, and from this a track led south-east across the field to Upper Eastcott Farm, and thence up Eastcott Hill to Old Swindon.

This bridge and track fixed the line of what was to become the next focus of private housing. During the 1850s terraces of small houses sprang up beside the track, which was then known along its whole length as Bridge Street. It was only later, during the 1860s and 1870s, that many of these houses were converted into shops, and then for the stretch of road south of Golden Lion Bridge a more stylish name, Regent Street, was coined to reflect its new commercial status. The principal crossroad of the modern pedestrianized shopping centre now marks the site of the Golden Lion, but a few of the 1850s workers' houses still peep from behind shopfronts towards the southern end of Regent Street.

Until the mid-1860s most of New Swindon, Regent Street apart, lay to the north of the Wilts and Berks Canal. Gooch's decision to build a rolling mill for iron rails at the works in 1861 attracted workers from the ironworks of South Wales. Initially they were housed with their families in the Barracks, but by 1864 a 'Welsh Colony' had been built for them between the railway village and Westcott Place. This was called Cambria Place, and had its own Welsh-speaking Baptist chapel. Further east, between the railway village and the angle formed by the junction of the North Wilts Canal with the Wilts and Berks, Sheppard's Field was built-up with the four roads of his name, John, Henry, Harding and Sheppard Streets.

It was a busy time for the railway works, as we have seen, with the new carriage works opening in 1868 and a full order book for locomotives continuing through much of the 1870s. These prosperous years, from about 1865 to 1877, found the property speculators and small-time builders busy too. Now a tide of red brick began to creep up the hill towards Old Swindon. Havelock Street and its neighbours now beneath the Brunel Centre were followed by the advance guard of terraces around what became Regent Circus and the present Swindon College. Infilling occurred in the area between the railway village and the canal, now occupied by Farnsby Street and the Murray John building. And forays were made eastward across the North Wilts Canal

Cambria Place, later and less familiar than the railway village, was built in the 1860s for Welsh ironworkers and their families.

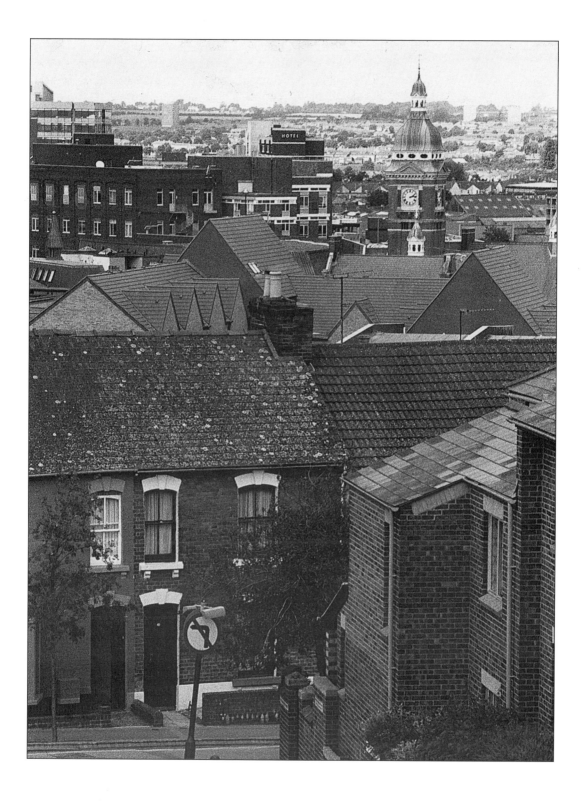

towards the station. But large areas of farmland around Swindon were out of bounds to the developer until 1885, because of a legal dispute over the inheritance of what remained of one of Swindon's former manors, the Vilett estate. This restriction led, not only to overcrowding on cramped sites which were available, but also to sporadic house-building in far-flung places, such as on the slopes of Kingshill, and north of the railway at Even Swindon and Gorse Hill.

At the works the wheels of progress ground to a halt in about 1877, as we have seen, and the influx of new population was stemmed. The housebuilding market did not revive until after 1885, by when the restriction on Vilett lands had been lifted. This enforced lull, whatever its economic consequences at the time, offered a pause for reflection. New Swindon, from being a chaotic jumble of uncontrolled accretions for the accommodation of railway workers, was developing into an important town, with its own commercial and retail areas, a form of local government (New Swindon Board of Health), and a variety of social and welfare activities provided by, or connected with, the main employer.

One consequence of this was that, when building recommenced after 1885, schemes were on a larger and grander scale. Three developments set out to alter the balance of Swindon. The first lay to the west of Regent Street and was centred on a new alignment, Commercial Road. The aim of the builders was to capture from Regent Street its trading supremacy. A market was built at its western end, where it met the canal, and at the eastern end Regent Circus was laid out by 1889, around a blatantly municipal building, the town hall of 1891. The second scheme involved forging a proper link with the old town by creating a thoroughfare up the hill. Victoria Road, as it was christened, was made up in 1888, and by 1900 houses and side streets had been built along much of its length. The third large-scale development, which took place during the years around 1900, filled with houses the area between the station and the canal, aligned on Manchester Road and Broad Street.

Alongside these giant modifications to the Swindon landscape the small opportunist builder continued his work of infilling odd plots and poking out into the suburbs. What is more – and this is often overlooked – Old Swindon too was growing, especially on its northern and western edges. Here, according to Betjeman, we shall encounter the Victorian middle classes: 'Outcast from the most exclusive sets of the Old Town, houses will be coming tripping down Eastcott Hill and Prospect Hill and the Bath Road on their way to New Swindon. Rising on the railway boom, the more fortunate of the mechanics will climb the hill to greet them.'

Opposite: The view across New Swindon from Dover Street on the hillside.

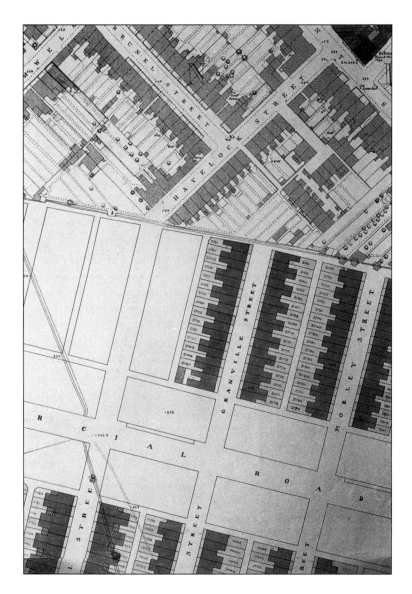

An extraordinary map in the Wiltshire Record Office, showing the power of a pre-railway boundary to affect the course of Swindon's development. The boundary is shown on the tithe map (see p. 62), and could not be transgressed until the Vilett estate became available in 1885. Thereafter a new street plan, based on Commercial Road, was adopted, disrupting the old layout as if a geological fault had come between them. The Ordnance Survey plan, published during the 1880s, has here been augmented by later manuscript additions showing the Commercial Road development.

In a poem written several years before his Swindon essay Betjeman described such houses as, 'brick-built breeding boxes of new souls'. To his subtle eye the little differences of detail and architectural gradations of Swindon houses from street to street and area to area reflect all the nuances of English social class. Bricks and mortar remain as mute evidence of the pretensions of their builders, and the aspirations of first and subsequent occupants. Observant pedestrians on their way down Victoria Road will notice such things; in particular they may

The house in Victoria Road where Richard Jefferies lived between 1875 and 1877. This drawing was published in 1896, in a posthumous collection of his local history essays.

Richard Jefferies, 1848–87, naturalist, novelist, lover of the Wiltshire countryside.

spot the plaque recording the fact that Richard Jefferies lived for a year in one of the houses.

Jefferies was a man of the countryside, not the town, and to categorize him on the basis of his house as an aspiring middle-class Victorian seems somehow inadequate. Born at Coate in 1848 he was one of the last of thousands of Swindonians to be baptized at the old parish church of Holy Rood (in January 1849) before its replacement by Christ Church in 1851. After a spell as a local journalist he supported himself and his family by writing novels and essays, until his premature death from tuberculosis in 1887. Interest in his work, never entirely extinguished, revived during the 1970s, and some of his books on country life and natural history are now regarded as classics of the genre. His output included work on local history, and we may claim him as Swindon's first historian, although this was not his forte. But, like Betjeman, he was interested in the sociology of the town, and his observations on Swindon in 1867 are astute.

Jefferies drew a distinction between 'the lower class of mechanics, especially the factory labourers', on the one hand, who were local men from the surrounding villages attracted to the works by higher wages; and the class of 'educated mechanics', on the other – well travelled, intelligent, eager to debate, read and learn. This latter group, 'in reality the protoplasm, or living matter, out of which modern society is evolved', were incomers to New Swindon, and their presence leavened the social life and character of the town. They ate meat and lived well, relatively speaking, but were not guilty of excesses; because they expected a regular income they tended to spend their money rather than save. This trait, in the eyes of Jefferies the farmer's son, was a grave character defect, but it resulted from a generous, liberal disposition, always ready to buy a friend a drink, take the family for a jaunt, or treat a daughter to a new dress. 'The mechanic does not set a value upon money in itself.'

This assessment accords precisely with F.H. Spencer's memory of his father, a precision engineer at the works who was descended from a Lancashire family of small landowners. A quiet, thoughtful man, 'with an unexhibited pride at the root of his nature', he had a passion for books, and for visiting abbeys and cathedrals to study their architecture. There was a second-hand piano in the house, and one of the children had a violin. But – and here Jefferies' stricture rings true – 'We were slightly in debt. The rent was always a few weeks in arrear, and there was an ancient butcher's bill incurred during the long stay of convalescent relatives in a distant past, which we gradually liquidated by occasional half-crowns.'

Spencer contrasts this household of culture, intellect and decency with the miserable condition of the rented house itself. This too has an echo in the observations of Jefferies. In one of his novels, *Greene Ferne Farm* published in 1880, we follow a curate about his visits in 'Kingsbury', alias New Swindon. 'At the end of a new street hastily "run up cheap" and "scamped", they found a large black pool, once a pond in the meadow, now a slough of all imaginable filth, at whose precipitous edge the roadway stopped abruptly.' Upstairs in one of these 'scamped' six-roomed houses, with doors that warped and would not shut, they visited a young man recuperating from an accident at the works, lying on his bed in a sickly, fetid room in the middle of a summer day. He was one of the 'lower class of mechanics' arrived from a nearby village, and had been an under-shepherd. Now from his squalid surroundings he was staring out at lambs in a nearby field through a window that could not be made to open.

We suggested earlier that, during the doldrums of the late 1870s when this description was written, New Swindon had a respite, and took stock of its progress before beginning to organize itself as a proper town. In fact some urban trappings had already been in place for a number of years. Shops, schools, pubs and chapels sprang up throughout the town in the wake of new housing, and supplemented the medical, recreational and cultural facilities associated with the GWR. And both old and new towns had had their separate boards of health since 1864. The New Swindon Local Board organized gas street lamps, and began a rudimentary sewerage system. Although this was gradually

Swindon Town Hall, built in 1891 as the offices of the New Swindon Local Board, and destined in 1900 to become the focus of a combined Old and New Swindon.

Swindon borough arms, granted in 1901. The town's staple industry was prominently represented.

improved and refined it continued for many years to demonstrate its shortcomings in various offensive ways, such as the slough of filth depicted by Jefferies. Later came a piped water supply from water-works at Wroughton, and various public health and protection measures followed.

During the early years the two town boards refused to co-operate with each other, but gradually commonsense prevailed, and matters of joint concern, such as firefighting, and the provision of a cemetery and an isolation hospital, were tackled together. During the building boom of the 1890s the conclusion became inevitable that Old and New Swindon should be governed together, and this was probably anticipated in the positioning of the New Swindon Local Board's offices at Regent Circus in 1891 – the town hall, as it became, was sited roughly halfway between the original nuclei of the two towns. During the 1890s amalgamation and incorporation as a borough became a burning local issue, and in 1897 the Privy Council was petitioned for Swindon to obtain its charter. On 9 November 1900, a little over sixty years after Gooch and Brunel had finished their picnic, the Borough of Swindon became a reality.

Evening Star and Sunrise

Gaslight in the living room, harmonium in the front parlour, and bowler hat hanging in the hall – the home life of the successful railway worker in about 1900 has been beautifully re-created at 34 Faringdon Road, the foreman's cottage which since 1980 has been the railway village museum. James Hall, a second-generation Swindon railwayman, lived there in modest comfort with his wife and family, in the house which his parents had moved into when it was new and he was a child, forty years before in about 1860.

Within a short stroll from his back door was (or in 1900 would shortly be) a bewildering range of services and facilities provided by

The Mechanics' Institute building in Emlyn Square, at the heart of the railway village and community. The drawing dates from 1914.

local government, 'the company', private enterprise and self-help. There were shops and pubs, a covered market and the mechanics' institute (with its enterprising range of social and cultural activities), churches and chapels, a hospital and swimming baths, and schools for the children. A theatre (the Queen's, later the Empire) had been built in 1898, some twenty working-men's clubs had opened between 1880 and 1900, professional football at the County Ground had begun in 1895, and there had been a local evening paper since 1882. A railway line linking Swindon with Andover and destinations in the South-East was built in 1881–3, and provided Old Town with its own station. A few years' later, in 1903, the new borough council would take over the running of its schools, and also begin university extension lectures. During the same year an electricity works was built, and it generated power not only for electric street lighting, but also for a tramway system which started running services in 1904.

Everything – all these trappings of successful urban growth – was a product of the previous sixty years, and had grown up with the railway works, on which it all still ultimately depended for its existence. But during the twentieth century new themes emerge – the decline and fall of the works; the industries which came to replace them; and the overspill world of the suburbs.

Swindon's electricity works was opened in Corporation Street in 1903. One of its main functions was to provide power for the tramway network.

The fate of the works may be gauged in statistics. The workforce had reached 14,000 by 1905, and peaked in 1925 at 14,369. In 1930 it was 11,500, and in 1939 10,500. After 1945 it remained fairly constant at about 10,000 until 1960, but had fallen to 8,000 in 1962, and 5,100 in 1967. A low point of 2,200 was reached in 1973, but thereafter it rose to 3,800 by 1980, before dropping to just over 1,000 before closure in 1986. It has been suggested that at the start of the century the GWR division based at Swindon, which was responsible for locomotives, carriages and wagons, as well as their drivers and firemen (a grand total of about 17,000 employees), was probably the largest undertaking in British, and perhaps European, industry at the time. With the opening of a new carriage store in 1938 the works reached their maximum geographical extent, more than 326 acres, including 79 acres roofed over.

Another way of looking at things is to consider the output of the works, and the legendary names of railway history responsible for designing and producing the famous locomotives built at Swindon. In 1901 G.J. Churchward, deputy and superintendent-elect, produced on a single sheet of paper the diagrams for six new types of locomotive, which employed a revolutionary boiler design. During his time in office (he retired as superintendent in 1921) five of these types went

Trams first ran in Swindon in September 1904, and this detail is taken from a view of the Bridge Street – Fleet Street junction on the first day of operation.

Part of a plan of the railway works in 1935, shortly before it reached its greatest extent.

into production; they became the GWR's workhorses, and earned enviable reputations for speed and reliability. Developments in carriage and wagon design also went on apace, and the ingenious designers and engineers in the works continued to show that they could turn their hand to any problem – in 1891 they had patented a cake-cutting machine for the annual children's fete, and in 1914 they built a pagoda-like advertising kiosk for use at agricultural shows, which still survives as a refreshment stall in the Town Gardens. Churchward played an influential part too in the life of the town. He was the borough's mayor in the year of incorporation, and its first honorary freeman. After his retirement he continued to live in a house near the railway works until his death (run down by an express train while examining a loose rail) in 1933.

C.B. Collett, Churchward's successor, was responsible for developing many of the most famous classes of GWR locomotive, including 'Castles', 'Kings', 'Granges', 'Manors' and 'Halls'. His term of office (1922–41) also included the first experiments with diesel traction. On

This refreshment pagoda in Town Gardens was made in the railway workshop as a GWR advertising kiosk.

1 January 1948 the GWR ceased to exist, and the nationalized British Railways took over the works, but steam locomotive production continued through the 1950s alongside new diesel-hydraulic units. The last steam locomotive to be built for British Railways emerged from the works on 18th March 1960, and was named *Evening Star*. Diesel-hydraulic traction was phased out during the 1960s in favour of diesel-electric; this jeopardized Swindon's future, and by 1970 it seemed likely that British Rail Engineering Ltd (as it had become) would close the works. The gloom was premature, and it was not until 1985, while Swindon was preparing to celebrate the 150th anniversary of the founding of the GWR, that closure was announced, with effect from 26 March 1986. Commemoration gave way to anger, and the celebrations were abandoned.

'I had never been to Swindon before, and all I knew about it was that the Great Western Railway had its chief works there and that it made the best railway engines in the world.' So wrote J.B. Priestley when he visited the town in 1933. It was quite true, of course, and

The Harding Street mural of a 'King' class locomotive, which was executed in 1985. Swindon's reputation for excellence in railway engineering was maintained between the wars by this and other designs, the work of C.B. Collett.

Swindon was proud of it. But civic pride had, by the 1930s, become tempered with a kind of malaise, which manifested itself in several ways. Priestley found the shops shoddy, the houses monotonous and the food in the eating-house dubious. As he trudged the damp, dark, autumnal town after dinner, and found it murky, with an unfriendly, shuttered look, he mused on 'these smaller industrial towns, where you can work but cannot really play'. Betjeman detected the same malaise in the new building of the inter-war years, which made Swindon, he said, look like any industrial suburb anywhere. And Kenneth Hudson, writing much later, during the 1960s, made himself very unpopular locally by suggesting that to the outside world, 'the name Swindon almost automatically conveyed the idea of somewhere out-of-date, small, mean and stick-in-the-mud,' and that this was, 'an important, if sad, part of the legacy of the railway town; it was a burden the town appeared to have to carry'. Hudson suggested a change of name to dispel the image, and provoked a storm of protest – yet Thamesdown Borough Council was less than a decade away.

An obvious explanation for the malaise is that it began when the works and the town stopped expanding at the phenomenal rate of the first sixty years. And it is precisely then, during the Edwardian years, that we first detect it, in a locally famous book, *Life in a Railway Factory*, by a locally famous author, Alfred Williams. Williams was a product of the mechanics' institute ethos of self-improvement for the working man by education. Poet, folksong collector, lover of the countryside, and student of ancient languages, he worked as a steam-hammerman at the works from 1893 until poor health ended his arduous career in 1914. He wrote his description of the works in 1911, but it was not published until 1915. It offers a detailed picture of the working environment, including all the dangers and hardships, the victimization and practical jokes. It is a powerful book by an embittered employee who, it must be admitted, is blatantly unsympathetic to the GWR. Much of the abuse and horseplay which he describes was harmless – apprentices, for instance, were misled by their older workmates into believing that they all had to be branded on the buttocks with the company initials, using a hot iron stamp. But Williams also described a deteriorating relationship between shopfloor and management, as new machinery was introduced, bureaucracy increased, and the quest for greater efficiency imposed ever stiffer burdens on the workforce.

This increased tension in labour relations (by no means unique to Swindon at this time) which the disaffected Alfred Williams chronicles in his book is reflected also in the growth of union membership. A Swindon Trades Council was formed in 1891 to represent the various unions in the town, and it claimed that its membership of 1,000 in 1892 and 2,000 in 1903 had risen by 1917 to 10,000. The Trades Council put up candidates to local councils, including one man, Reuben George, who went on to become mayor and alderman of Swindon, and a county councillor, dying in 1936. A larger-than-life character, and champion of the Workers' Educational Association, he has become one of Swindon's folk-heroes, along with the philanthropic rag-and-bone man, James 'Raggy' Powell, and David Murray John, town clerk from 1937 to 1974. In complete contrast to the shabby image Swindon may have had among outsiders, their whole-hearted commitment to the town has given it a tangible civic pride and dignity which has become a notable feature of its twentieth-century history.

As expansion and prosperity at the works became less dependable during and after the First World War, the borough and trades councils realized that Swindon had to diversify, and attract new industries into the town. Early arrivals – the clothing workshops already described, as well as Wills' tobacco factory in 1915, and Garrard Engineering in

BOROUGH OF SWINDON: ELECTION OF MAYOR AND ALDERMEN : NOVEMBER 1903 :
HINTON 31 . HILL 27 . POWELL 28 . GEORGE 23 CHURCHWARD 22 WHEELER 22
(MAYOR)
MR COUNCILLOR COOK INVESTS THE MAYOR

This caricature of prominent Swindon councillors includes Reuben George, James 'Raggy' Powell, and G.J. Churchward.

1919 – were all chiefly employers of women, so did not provide a direct substitute for the railway works. In fact as numbers at the works began to decline during the 1930s many engineering workers found employment at Morris Motors in Cowley, Oxford, and commuted there from Swindon by train on a daily basis. The Second World War brought aircraft and engineering factories to the Swindon area, including several large concerns – Vickers Armstrong, Plessey and R.A. Lister – which stayed on afterwards. Such were the employment opportunities in the town during the war, in fact, that immigration had to be limited, and Swindon was designated a closed area which civilians could not enter without permission.

Three new elements emerged after the war to complicate the process of expansion and diversification. First was the development of forward planning at local and national level. This meant that the opportunist piecemeal growth of the town in response to the needs of employers was a thing of the past. Second was the problem that Swindon, within its existing boundaries, was full-up, and any further expansion would encroach on the neighbouring local authority – Highworth Rural District Council – and affect Wiltshire County Council. The long-standing antipathy between Swindon and the rest of Wiltshire still awaits its historian. Third was government policy, which at first favoured the creation of new towns, but after 1951 preferred the controlled growth of existing centres as 'overspill' towns. Swindon was designated a London overspill town on 25 June 1952, and this had a profound effect on its subsequent development.

The industrial and employment consequences, with which we are now concerned, were that numerous engineering, electrical, scientific and distributive companies opened plants in and around Swindon during the 1950s and 1960s, including one, Pressed Steel, which by 1965 had a larger workforce at its Stratton premises than the railway works. By 1970, encouraged in particular by the borough council's vigorous promotion of itself to potential employers, there were over 35,000 manufacturing jobs in Swindon. Many were located in units on council-initiated trading and industrial estates. Expansion continued during the 1970s, although the main growth now was in service and white-collar industries. A temporary check during the early 1980s has been followed by a dramatic upturn in Swindon's fortunes, especially in the so-called 'sunrise' industries, of computers, electronics and information technology. The startling architecture of Swindon's 1980s new image includes futuristic warehouses, and even a windmill, which has been removed from Chiseldon and rebuilt to preside over a business park. It now greets the visitor along the western access road from the motorway – the motorway (opened in 1971) which has been one of modern Swindon's chief progenitors.

Hand in hand with the town's policy of diversification – so successful that even the site of the former railway works is being diversified with offices and enterprises of all kinds – has been the suburbanization of Swindon, and this must be the final theme of this summary of recent history. In chapter five we left Swindon in around 1900 at the point where the two towns had coalesced, and redbrick had sprawled haphazardly around them in most directions. But Swindon's Victorian housing development was not really suburban, rather it was a series of small accretions and piecemeal infillings, often on rather cramped sites. This process continued until 1914, with new housing concentrated on the Okus, Kingshill and quarry areas west of Old Town, the Broad Street district near the station, and north of the tracks at Gorse Hill and Even Swindon. After the First World War Swindon began to march out into the countryside.

Opposite: Western Street. Swindon College and modern office blocks jostle the town hall's proud tower for pride of place on the Swindon skyline.

Redcliffe Street, Even Swindon, in about 1905.

During the 1920s and 1930s, here as everywhere, there were two types of housing, council and private. In general terms council houses were sturdier, built to better specifications, and more imaginatively positioned on estates. The overriding concern for private house-builders and occupiers was that their houses should not look like council houses; in other respects economies were made, and this included so-called ribbon development along existing main roads, which saved expense on building the infrastructure of estate roads and services. Swindon expanded northwards, with a council estate at Pinehurst, and private housing at Rodbourne. The Pinehurst estate was laid out on a circular plan by one of the pioneers of the garden city movement, Sir Raymond Unwin (although he was not responsible for the design of the houses), and its tree-named streets were gradually built up between the wars. In addition to the Rodbourne estate private housing ribboned along the main roads radiating from Old Town. In 1928 much of the ancient parish of Rodbourne Cheney was absorbed within the borough boundary, and part of Stratton St Margaret was taken as well.

Swindon's population in 1901, we recall, was 45,000, and this had been a ninefold increase during the previous fifty years. By 1951 it had reached 69,000 – a substantial increase, but on nothing like the scale of the nineteenth century. Decade by decade between 1901 and 1951 the average growth was less than 10 per cent, a comfortable rate

The prospect north-eastwards from the Lawns across Walcot to Greenbridge. Private housing, local authority housing beyond, an industrial estate in the distance, and open country on the horizon. A typical view of post-war overspill Swindon.

The Link Centre at West Swindon, with De Vere Hotels beyond. West Swindon has become a laboratory for striking and contrasting 1980s architectural styles.

of expansion which these suburban adventures could readily accommodate. But after 1945, and especially after the London overspill decision in 1952, the rate of growth increased again, with a consequent need for carefully planned suburban expansion. Between 1951 and 1961 another 23,000 people came to live in Swindon, nearly as many in ten years as in the previous fifty. But they were only the tip of an anticipated iceberg. Plans produced during the 1960s envisaged growth to 180,000, 200,000, 230,000, even 400,000 by the end of the century. The 200,000 estimate, suggested in 1968, became the accepted target.

Until the 1952 decision, Swindon's post-war housing effort had been concentrated, as before, to the north of the town. To these years principally belong the suburbs of Moredon and Penhill. But from 1952 a massive expansion to the east began. Walcot East and Walcot West came first, separated not only by a new dual-carriageway road, Queen's Drive of 1953, but also by the English class system, which still endeavoured to distinguish between council and private houses. Next came private housing at Lawn, and council housing at Park North and South. And with them, in the early 1960s, Swindon's boundaries were full up again, and further expansion had to encroach on its neighbours. Meanwhile those neighbours were themselves growing rapidly. The two rural districts bordering Swindon (Cricklade and Wootton Bassett, and Highworth) grew by a total of nearly 20,000

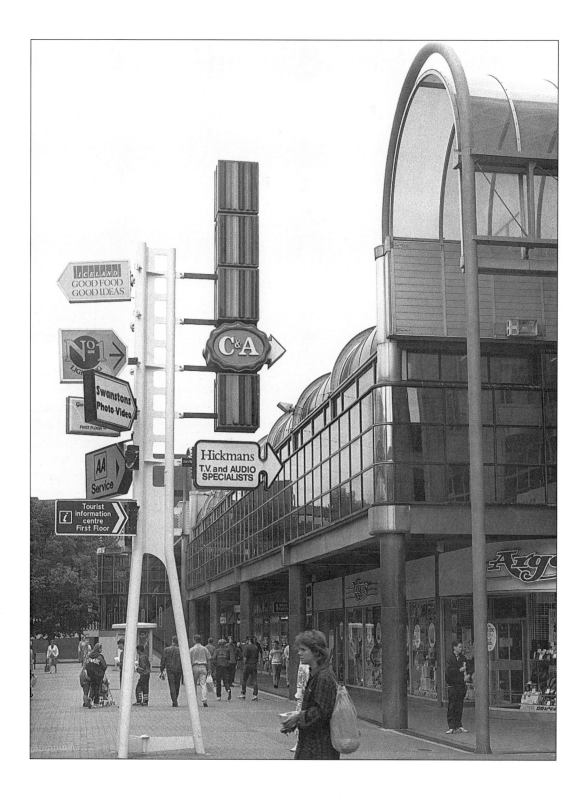

Opposite: Canal Walk, in the heart of Swindon's Brunel shopping centre. As its name suggests, this pedestrian street follows the line of the Wilts and Berks Canal.

The David Murray John Tower, twenty-two storeys high. It commemorates Swindon's influential town clerk, who died in 1974, shortly after Swindon as a borough had ceased to exist.

population between 1951 and 1966, and one parish, Stratton St Margaret, returned a population of 19,400 at the 1971 census, which was larger than most Wiltshire towns.

The key planning document of the 1960s, the so-called 'silver report', spawned further suburban housing and industrial expansion. Initially this was concentrated to the east, at Liden, Nythe, Covingham, Dorcan and Eldene, where gradual infilling took place up to the line of the Stratton St Margaret by-pass (our old friend the Roman road). But during the 1980s an entirely new area was opened up west of Swindon, and this was developed as a self-contained community, with its own facilities. Meanwhile radical changes were taking place in the town centre, as Victorian cottages were demolished to make way for pedestrianized shopping precincts. After West Swindon of the 1980s, Haydon in the north-west is set to become the growth point of the 1990s. But that is for the historian of the future.

It is too early to assess in historical terms the social impact of Swindon's recent growth. But when in the fulness of time another chapter comes to be written, a good starting point will be the study commissioned from Kenneth Hudson in 1964/5, which was published in 1967. It is a sociological survey of Swindon at the 100,000 mark, *An Awkward Size for a Town*, and it describes in great detail the living standards and aspirations of 1960s Swindonians. The dowdy image of the railway terraces had not then been shaken off, the shopping malls of the town centre were not complete, the Wyvern Theatre had not been built, the 'hi-tech' industries were decades away, the railway works were still a powerful force. Replying to a questionnaire about his ambitions, a sixth-former replied in terms of the initials he wanted to see after his name – BSc, PhD, FRS, OBE, – 'and having made this clear, said he doubted if Swindon was going to be big enough to hold him'. Swindon is a good deal bigger now, intellectually as well as geographically. I wonder, twenty-something years on, whether he achieved his ambitions, and whether he still lives in Swindon.

S = START

The route shown indicates
both the longer and the
shorter walks. Where the
route divides, follow the
dashed line if the shorter
walk is preferred.

Based on the ORDNANCE SURVEY maps with the permission of the controller of H.M. Stationery Office. Crown copyright.

Old and New Swindon

T his walk begins at the Market Square in Old Town, and after exploring the hilltop settlement descends by Eastcott Hill to New Swindon. From Regent Street it follows the course of the canal to Cambria Place and the railway village, ending at Fleming Way, from where a regular bus service runs back up to Old Town. Pay and display car parking is available close to the start of the walk. An option to shorten the tour, by exploring Old Town only, is indicated in the text; readers wishing to confine their walk to New Swindon should begin at Regent Circus on p. 102. Pedestrian crossings and road crossings with dropped kerbs are used wherever possible, and possible difficulties and alternatives for wheelchair users are described.

Throughout this tour instructions about the route are given in bold. The paragraph(s) of description which follow instructions usually relate to features visible at points along this part of the route, so should be read while carrying out the instruction.

The Market Square, now a small car park, was probably laid out during the thirteenth century, as part of an attempt to turn the settlement at Swindon into a market town. High Street, which adjoins it on its west side, as well as Wood Street and Newport ('the new market') Street, are probably also part of this exercise in medieval town planning. The market seems not to have flourished until it was revived after 1626, but thereafter it competed with Highworth as the principal cattle market in north-east Wiltshire. This revitalized market place had a covered market cross in the centre, which was demolished in 1793.

In common with many other small towns at the time, Swindon in the nineteenth century tried to make its market more attractive for farmers and corn dealers. A market house was begun on the south side

87

Old Town market square
with town hall and corn
exchange tower in 1923.

of the square in 1852, replacing a depot for long-distance waggons
(which the railway had made redundant). This market house is the
classical building seen to the right of the tower, but although its
upper floor was used for its intended purpose as a town hall, the
ground floor never became a covered market, and its arches were
filled in for shops. Instead a new corn exchange with an Italianate
tower was built to the left of it in 1864–6. After some fifty years the
building became a skating rink and later a cinema and bingo hall.
The motto over the door, 'Blessed be the Lord who daily loadeth us
with benefits' is perhaps more appropriate to a corn exchange than
to a bingo hall.

Opposite these buildings of Bath and Swindon stone, on the north
side is a smart eighteenth-century brick house, Square House (now
bank offices). And to the east runs Dammas Lane, which was formerly
built up with small houses. The name is supposed to derive from
damsons, as the lane led to the manor house orchards. The adjacent
Saxon Court, a recent housing development, occupies the area in
which Saxon huts were discovered and excavated, and so may represent the centre of the settlement which preceded medieval Swindon.

Face the corn exchange and walk along the lane (The Planks) which skirts it on the left. By the car park entrance turn left and continue for about 100 yards, past the auction rooms, until the lane bears right in front of a tree-lined grassed area. Here turn left and walk up the path into the public park known as the Lawn. Explore the remains of the manor house gardens adjoining the locked churchyard of Holy Rood on your right. (Wheelchair users will find it easier to turn right from the Market Square into High Street, and then turn right again between ornamental gate piers along the path to the Lawn. The churchyard is away to the right.)

The Planks is supposedly derived from a dialect name for flagstones, and it leads towards the site of a mill demolished in about 1860. The mill, which stood below the churchyard, was fed by a spring called Church Well and turned by an extremely large overshot wheel standing more than thirty feet high. The spring was also used as a water supply, and still feeds the lakes which lie at the southern end of the Lawn, below the church.

The Lawn from the west in about 1900.

'The Lawn' is the name given not only to the area of wooded landscape parkland which separates Old Swindon from the twentieth-century suburbs of Lawn, Park and Walcot, but was also used for the manor house which stood within it until it was demolished in 1952. A sunken garden survives with balustrades, which lay immediately west of the house. The house itself was of brick and stone, and rather similar in style to a surviving house (42, Cricklade Street) which we shall see presently. The Lawn was earlier called Swindon House, and was until 1931 the home of the Goddard family, manorial owners of High Swindon. It presumably occupied the site of the principal (or demesne) house of Swindon's medieval owners before the planned town was created in the thirteenth century.

The adjoining churchyard contains the chancel and part of the nave arcade of Holy Rood Church. This was Swindon's parish church from the middle ages until 1851, when Christ Church was completed. The author Richard Jefferies was baptized here in 1849. By this date it consisted of a mixture of medieval work and eighteenth-century repairs. But the whole structure was in poor repair – 'hopelessly out of condition, and there being really nothing worth restoring', according to an author who remembered it very well – so that the new church was built, and most of Holy Rood, including its tower, was demolished. Its chancel, however, was made weatherproof, and the nave arcades were retained, probably so as to give a picturesque view from the mansion windows. Occasional services are still held in the chancel, and parties can be shown around on request.

Our tour will leave the Lawn now but, if time permits, a stroll around the parkland to see the lakes, the avenue or 'Long Walk' where

Holy Rood Church in 1847, when it was still in use. It has been suggested that this is the oldest photograph of Swindon to exist. It was taken by a friend of Fox Talbot of Lacock, who had invented the negative – positive process five years earlier.

Gideon Mantell walked with his 'first love', and since his day the view across suburban Swindon, will be amply rewarded.

From the churchyard area walk towards the eighteenth-century brick gazebo tower, and about halfway between them you will encounter a substantial path. Turn left along this and follow it to the exit from the Lawn, which is by a long avenue. This emerges into High Street between a pair of ornamental gatepiers. Stop at this point to examine the architecture of the street.

We have suggested that the area between the former manor house, the churchyard and the market square is probably the site of the Saxon and early medieval village of Swindon. The market square and High Street represent a planned addition, tacked on to the west of the village. Although the present buildings lining the High Street are not medieval they occupy sites within rectangular tenements which were probably laid out during the thirteenth century. The avenue which takes us back to High Street presumably occupies one such tenement. It was created as the main entrance into the Goddard's park, and originally had lodge houses on each side, as well as the surviving gatepiers.

The row of buildings opposite, along the western side of High Street, dates from the sixteenth to the nineteenth century, and is typical north Wiltshire small-town architecture. From left to right, the Bell has a Victorian facade with a huge bell, but retains traces of an earlier galleried inn behind, and claims to date from 1515. Three doors along, at No. 16, notice 'GH' and the date 1631 on the rain-water heads. Old Town Court, now Barclays, proclaims 'Bowly Brewer' above its semi-circular arch. During the 1860s Bowly took over the North Wilts Brewery, behind High Street, from John Henry Harding Sheppard, who gave his four names to streets built on his land in New Swindon which we shall encounter later. No. 4, Eastcott House is on the site of the former King of Prussia Inn, demolished in 1981; Limmex, on the corner, has a date of 1708 and the letters 'MH'.

From the gatepiers turn right along High Street, and cross by the pedestrian crossing. Continue to the corner, cross Wood Street, and carry straight on down the hill until you find yourself opposite the entrance to Christ Church. Read the following paragraphs as you go.

Opposite the junction with Wood Street stands Old Swindon's principal inn, the Goddard Arms. The site had earlier been occupied by one of the town's manor houses, and then a thatched inn called the Crown. The present creeper-clad building dates from the eighteenth century. The character of Wood Street is that of a successful Victorian shopping street, and derives from the prosperity which accrued to Old Town traders during the mid-nineteenth century, before New Swindon had developed its own shopping streets. A directory of 1848 claimed that Old Swindon's shops were 'assuming an appearance equal to those of Bath and Cheltenham'. But a few years earlier it had been lined by poor labourers' thatched cottages and blacksmith's forges, producing intolerable noise and smoke, according to Jefferies. It was sometimes called Blacksmith's Street, or alternatively Windmill Street, because of a windmill which occupied a site near the King's Arms. On the corner the former Wilts and Dorset Bank building of 1884 occupies the site of Blackford's butcher's shop. Members of the Blackford family were champion backsword players, a game which involved clubbing an opponent's head with a wooden stick until the blood ran one inch.

Beyond the Wood Street junction the road continues northward as Cricklade Street, although its old name was Brock Hill. It soon begins to descend the hillside, and a long view over Swindon's northern suburbs opens up. Until a fatal coaching accident in the early nineteenth century the road was carried more abruptly over the brow of the hill,

Wood Street in about 1900.
The Goddard Arms in High
Street closes the vista.

on a level with the present pavement on the Christ Church side. After the accident the gradient was eased for the safety of wheeled vehicles, but not without complaints from the owner of the grand house at the top of the hill. This, No. 42 Cricklade Street (now Townsend's, Solicitors), is generally regarded as the finest piece of domestic architecture in Swindon. Sir John Betjeman called it 'one of the most distinguished town houses in Wiltshire'. It was built in 1729, and was occupied as a private house by members of leading Swindon families, including Harding and Vilett, before becoming the county court and offices.

Further down the hill an inscription records a bequest by Alexander Anderson which paid for a group of four almshouses next to the churchyard in 1877. Christ Church was designed by Sir George Gilbert Scott in Midlands Decorated style, and was opened in 1851. The hillside site was donated by Ambrose Goddard, lord of the manor,

Christ Church, drawn in 1914. The noble Victorian building replaced Holy Rood in 1851.

and the lofty spire, which is such a prominent feature of the Swindon townscape, was copied from the genuinely medieval spire at Buckworth near Huntingdon. 'So new, so high, so pure, so broach'd, so tall', it presides over the peal of ten bells celebrated by Betjeman in a poem.

Opposite Christ Church turn left into Church Road, which later becomes Union Row. When this emerges into the main road (Victoria Road) turn left, cross by the pedestrian crossing, and make your way back up towards Old Town. At the T-junction and mini-roundabout at the top of Victoria Road follow the pavement around to the right, so that you find yourself in the garden of Apsley House, Swindon Museum.

The siting of Christ Church on Brock Hill must have improved the status of what had been the poor end of Old Swindon. A street of meagre cottages called Little London ran down from the west end of Wood Street to join Brock Hill where it bends shortly below Christ

Little London, here seen in about 1912, was one of the poorer quarters of Old Swindon.

Church. This is no longer built up, and now has the appearance of a back alley. Church Road crosses it, and then meets Albert Street, which retains some of its 1840s stone cottages, but not its notorious pub, the Rhinoceros Inn, which stood at this crossing until it was demolished in 1963. Albert Street and Victoria Street (as the upper end of Victoria Road was originally known) result from Old Swindon's growth during the 1840s, and are the counterpart of the railway village at the foot of the hill. If, when you have crossed the pedestrian crossing in Victoria Road, you look back across the road, you will see a quite distinguished terrace of stone houses (as opposed to the later and meaner brick houses beyond the Union Row turning). On No. 93 at first floor level a plaque records that this was the home of Richard Jefferies, the Wiltshire naturalist and country writer, from 1875–7.

Walking up Victoria Road to its junction it is important to realise that, despite its present importance as the main road between Old and New Swindon, this link was not established until about 1875, as the towns began to coalesce. Earlier ways down the hill were by Brock Hill and Little London, as we have seen, and by Eastcott Hill, which we shall use later. Victoria Street ended merely in a footpath across fields, by way of Prospect (beyond the present BBC Wiltshire Sound building).

At the top of Victoria Road, as our footpath leads us round the corner into Bath Road, it is time to take stock. Swindon's medieval street plan was roughly a square of four streets. We have walked along the eastern side of this square (High Street), and looked along Wood Street, the northern side. Now we are at the north-western corner, and the western side is represented by Devizes Road. This was known as Short Hedge or Horse Fair until the nineteenth century, and was not built up to any great extent. But we are standing at pre-Victorian Swindon's growth point. Between the 1820s and 1850 housing had begun to creep from this junction southward along Devizes Road, northward along Victoria Street, and westward along what was then called The Sands, but is now Bath Road. Among the first of the new arrivals (probably by 1830) was Apsley House, which has been home to Swindon Museum since 1930. A larger and later development was Bath Terrace, the long row of shops opposite the top of Victoria Road.

Swindon Museum and Art Gallery includes interesting displays of local history, archaeology and palaeontology, as well as important fine art and ceramics collections. Admission is free.

Looking eastward towards Wood Street in about 1920 from the middle of Bath Road outside Swindon Museum (not now a recommended vantage point). The buildings in the foreground have been demolished, and the road junction has been widened.

Walk along Bath Road, keeping on the right hand side until you reach the Methodist Church.

Bath Road is the fashionable nineteenth-century extension to Old Swindon, and its houses display a pleasing variety of styles, using brick, local stone, and occasionally Bath stone. After Apsley House the earliest are the attractive brick houses (now offices) with cast-iron porches, Nos. 8–14; they date from about 1835, and so are pre-railway. But on the other side of the road, and further along on both sides, the villas are decidedly Victorian, and mostly date from the 1850s and 1860s. The chapel was opened in 1880, and replaced earlier buildings in the Planks.

At this point there is a choice. If you intend to continue the tour by walking down the hill and exploring New Swindon, stay on the right hand side of Bath Road and walk to the corner of Eastcott Road. Resume the description on p. 99 below. If, however, you wish to postpone New Swindon for another occasion

and to return to the starting point at the Market Square, cross
the road by the pedestrian crossing just beyond the chapel, and
continue along Bath Road (away from Old Town) until you
reach Quarry Road. Turn left down Quarry Road and, after
about 100 yards, enter the Town Gardens by green iron gates

The botanical and horticultural pleasures of the Town Gardens are
beyond the scope of this guide, but their historical interest lies in their
origins as quarries. The gardens, and the surrounding residential streets,
occupy the area of medieval Swindon's Great Field. From the seventeenth century quarries were opened up in parts of this field, at first to
win Purbeck limestone, and later the Portland stone with which much of
Old Swindon is built. Quarrying declined in the later nineteenth century,

Town Gardens, on the site of
quarries, retains a nostalgic
late-Victorian ambience.
Here the rustic bridge is
depicted in about 1905.

and the Town Gardens were laid out as a public park in 1894. Their design makes full and attractive use of the different levels which resulted from quarrying activities. Near the bandstand is a polygonal refreshment kiosk. This was built by the GWR in Swindon works in 1914 for advertising purposes at local shows, and later sold to the borough council.

Make your way through the park to its main entrance in Westlecot Road. Cross the road and turn left. Walk along Westlecot Road until you reach the parapet of a railway bridge, and see the deep railway cutting below you. Unless you are a wheelchair user (in which case continue along Westlecot and Springfield Roads, left into Croft Road, right into Newport Street, and so back to the start), turn right into Bowling Green Lane, and immediately you will find a footpath sloping down the side of the cutting. On the floor of the cutting turn back sharp right, so that you walk under the railway bridge. Continue in the cutting, and under another bridge, until you emerge into a small industrial estate.

The Midland and South-Western Junction Railway station at Old Town, seen from the Devizes Road Bridge in 1913.

You are walking along part of the Midland and South Western Junction Railway line, which ran from near Cheltenham to Andover. This portion, with a station serving Old Town known as Swindon Town, was opened in 1881–2, and closed in 1961; the site of the station has become the industrial estate, and a mural painting reminds us of its former use. While walking in the cutting look for exposures of Swindon stone.

> **Take a left turn (Dewell Mews) out of the industrial estate, and through an estate of new houses, which have been built on the site of the cattle market. You will emerge into Marlborough Road next to a bronze statue of a ram. Turn left, and the town hall, corn exchange and Market Square are on your right. This is a convenient place to stop for those who want a shorter tour.**
>
> **The tour to New Swindon resumes at the corner of Bath Road and Eastcott Road. Turn right into Eastcott Road and follow it as it bends around the bus depot and begins to descend the hill. At this point it becomes Eastcott Hill. Cross to the left hand side of Eastcott Hill before you reach the main road at the bottom (Crombey Street), so that you can use the pedestrian crossing.Once across Crombey Street continue along the last short stretch of Eastcott Hill. Cross Commercial Road with care (it has no pedestrian crossing at this point, and is a fast and busy one-way street) and stop in front of the town hall in Regent Circus**

The descent down Eastcott Hill two hundred years ago would have taken us from the limestone hill of small-town Swindon, with its arable fields and its quarries, down to the flat, sparsely populated, clay pasturelands on the valley floor. This area, the northern portion of Swindon parish, was generally known as Eastcott, and was farmed from Upper and Lower Eastcott Farms. Upper Eastcott Farm stood close to the later Regent Circus, and had a small hamlet of cottages around it; Lower Eastcott Farm lay beyond Fleming Way beneath the site of the present bus station. Eastcott Road and Eastcott Hill preserve the course (including the bend) of the lane which connected Swindon with Eastcott, and provided the main link between Old and New Swindon until Victoria Road was created in about 1875.

During the later nineteenth century the houses of New Swindon spread southward up the hill towards the old town, and Old Swindon expanded northward to meet them. Until 1900 the two communities were administered separately, and the boundary between them crossed at the point where Eastcott Road (Old Swindon) turns into Eastcott Hill (New Swindon). Therefore the first side streets which we encounter – King William Street, South Street and North Street on our right, Lansdown Road on our left – are all part of Old Swindon's growth, and date from about 1870. North Street, as its name suggests, marks the northern limit of Old Swindon. But the next streets on our left – Brunswick, Pembroke and Savernake Streets – do not need to respect the boundary because they are a piece of later infilling; they date from 1906–7, after the two towns had amalgamated.

As we descend the hill the small streets to our right date from the 1870s and 1880s, and on our left we encounter Stafford Street and Dixon Street. As a speculative venture they were planned and laid out in 1873, but fell victim to the recession at the works and in the country, and were only patchily built up until the late 1880s. As soon as we pass the end of Dixon Street, however, we emerge from the recession, and find ourselves in a much larger piece of town development, result-

In 1886, when this Ordnance Survey plan was published, open country remained between Old and New Swindon, and Eastcott Hill, rather than the new Victoria Road, was the most important thoroughfare between them.

Opposite: (above) Looking northwards down Regent Street in 1902. The classical portico of the Baptist Tabernacle, built in 1886, was demolished in 1977–8; (below) Regent Street in 1912, looking south.

ing from the boom of the 1890s. The parallel Crombey Street and Commercial Road were the linchpins of the scheme, and numerous short residential roads lead off them at right angles. At the point where Commercial Road and Regent Street would have intersected Regent Circus was laid out, and this, with its imposing brick town hall of 1890–1, was Swindon in its most confident and optimistic mood. But not over-confident, it should be made clear – the original plan, to call it Trafalgar Square, was rejected as being too pretentious.

The town hall was designed in 'Danish Renaissance' style by an architect from Ipswich, Brightwen Binyon, and was originally built as the offices of the New Swindon Local Board. It became the headquarters of Swindon Borough Council when it was incorporated in 1900, but was replaced by new Civic Offices in Euclid Street in 1938. Since 1949 it has housed the central public library (Swindon Divisional Library), and now includes also the Town Hall Studio.

From Regent Circus walk down Regent Street, since 1975 largely pedestrianized, as far as the crossroad with the Parade and Canal Walk.

Regent Street began life as a track through fields, which connected the hamlet of Eastcott (in the Regent Circus and Theatre Square area) with the Golden Lion Bridge across the canal. Its first building was a Primitive Methodist Chapel, which opened near the Eastcott end in 1849; a later brick hall behind its site may still be seen down an alleyway on the left. During the 1850s terraces of small brick houses were built along this track, and it was regarded as a continuation of Bridge Street. F.H. Spencer, whom we encountered in chapter five, was born in one such terrace, York Place, which is now concealed behind shopfronts facing Regent Circus. As Swindon grew, so there was the need for a more convenient shopping centre than Old Town on the hill, and during the 1870s and 1880s most of the houses along this part of Bridge Street were converted to shops; to emphasise its new importance it was renamed Regent Street after the famous London street.

As you walk down Regent Street look above the alluring modern shopfronts. At the upper end of the street, and especially opposite Woolworth's, the roofs of the original small houses may be seen, and

Opposite: Regent Street was originally built up with small terraced houses in the 1850s, but from about 1870 onwards premises were converted piecemeal to retail use. Most of the houses have disappeared, but some of these depicted in 1860 (above) can still be seen behind the present-day shop façades opposite Woolworth's (below),

The replica golden lion in Canal Walk, near the site of Golden Lion Bridge and Inn (see p. 64).

there is a pleasant variety of later architectural styles. Notice, for instance, the name W.W. Hunter picked out in ornamental brickwork; he was a furniture dealer at the turn of the century, who also built two roads, Hunters Grove and St Mary's Grove (his wife was Mary), north of the railway line.

Beyond Edgeware Road much of Regent Street has been redeveloped in recent years, and the left hand side forms part of the Brunel Centre, which was opened in 1972. The pedestrian crossroad marks the site of the Golden Lion Inn, with its bridge across the Wilts and Berks Canal. The line of the canal is preserved by Canal Walk and the Parade, and a replica golden lion statue, erected in 1978, stands nearby. Near the lion, at the entrance to the adjacent shop, notice a stone canal milestone (now a listed building), which gives the distance to Semington, 26 miles. Semington, near Melksham, is the point at which the Wilts and Berks Canal joined the Kennet and Avon. The Parade, as

How many shoppers notice this relic of an earlier Swindon in Canal Walk? Semington was the western end of the Wilts and Berks Canal.

envisaged during the 1950s, was intended as a road for vehicles, but this plan was abandoned during the vogue for separating pedestrians and traffic which emerged around 1960, and so it was developed during the early 1960s as Swindon's first pedestrian precinct.

> **Having walked down Regent Street turn left along Canal Walk, and keep going. Do not be alarmed that your path takes you through and under a multi-storey car park, and under two road bridges. Continue until you reach the next bridge, Cambria Bridge, which is recognisable by the murals of canal scenes.**

The Wilts and Berks Canal, as we saw in chapter three, was built to link the Bristol and Bath area with the River Thames and London. The Swindon portion was completed in 1804 and the canal was opened throughout in 1810. At that time, and for several decades afterwards, the stretch along which you are walking passed open countryside on both sides, with only a distant view of civilization in the shape of Old Swindon on the hill to the left. During the development of New Swindon after 1840 the canal acted as a barrier, and influenced the way in which the street plan evolved. By the 1890s the canal's useful life was over, and its course through Swindon was both an inconvenience and a health hazard. In 1914 Swindon Borough Council

The derelict canal in 1914. The photographer was standing looking west at the junction of the Wilts and Berks with the North Wilts Canal, near the present pedestrian subway beneath Fleming Way. The Golden Lion Bridge, without its footbridge, can be seen in the distance.

purchased the Swindon portion, together with Coate Water, and the canal's course through the town was filled in.

This stretch of the walk provides a good illustration of how modern Swindon's shopping centre has been superimposed on the earlier pattern of residential streets and small terraced houses. Between Regent Street and the car park all is brash and modern, the shopfronts reflecting the 1970s Brunel Plaza and the office block, the 22-storey Murray John Tower. But beyond the car park and road bridges is a world of private back gardens and Victorian brick. The smaller, earlier houses are to the right of the canal; to the left Curtis Street and its neighbours date from the building boom of the more affluent 1890s, and their houses are consequently larger and better appointed.

> **Do not walk under Cambria Bridge, but instead turn right into Cambria Bridge Road, and shortly left into Cambria Place. Halfway along, noting Cambria Baptist Chapel to your left, turn right and you will emerge into Faringdon Road, opposite the former GWR Park.**

The tour now moves away from the canal to the world of the early railway settlement. We saw in chapter five that a rolling mill for iron rails was built at the works in 1860–1. To construct and operate it workmen from South Wales were encouraged to move with their families to Swindon. At first they were accommodated in the former lodging-house known as the Barracks, but by 1864 two rows of stone cottages, Cambria Place and Cambria Buildings (the south side of Faringdon Road), had been built for them. The project, which has been dubbed 'the second railway village', was perhaps financed by a block mortgage from a building society; at the heart of the community was the Welsh-speaking Baptist chapel, opened in 1866.

When this Welsh colony was established the line of Faringdon Road already existed, and had done for centuries as a track called the 'Fleetway'; indeed private housing was already springing up along it further to the west. To the north of 'Fleetway' a field was given to the GWR by the lord of Eastcott manor in 1844 in order to create a cricket ground and park, and this became the venue every August for a children's fete of gigantic proportions. The park was given by the GWR to the borough council in 1925, in exchange for land elsewhere which the company needed in order to extend the works. Beyond the park is visible the spire of St Mark's Church. This church was completed in 1845,

Cambria Place Baptist Chapel was built in 1866 and closed in 1986.

The children's fête held annually in the GWR Park. This photograph was taken in 1919 or 1920, so these children would now be approaching or have recently passed their eightieth birthdays.

and became the centre of Anglican worship for the railway village and burgeoning new town.

> **Turn right and walk along the right hand side of Faringdon Road until you have crossed Maxwell Street. Use the pedestrian crossing to cross Faringdon Road, and continue along the left hand side. The terraces of stone cottages which make up the railway village are now on your left, and in due course you will arrive at the centrepiece of the village, Emlyn Square.**

The circumstances and evolution of Swindon railway village are described in chapter four, especially pp. 47–53, and need not be repeated here. Having refreshed your memory you should stroll around the village, noting especially the lack of uniformity of detail between one terrace and another, the areas of more prestigious housing at the ends of terraces, the rear alleys (partly necessitated by the lack

These imposing buildings fronting Emlyn Square housed (from left to right) a temperance coffee house, the offices of the temperance society, and the Gluepot public house. The Murray John Tower protrudes above a railway village cottage.

of mains drainage and sewerage when they were built), and the larger communal buildings in and around Emlyn Square, such as the currently disused mechanics' institute. If time permits, a visit to the railway museum (the former Barracks), with its 'Return to Swindon' exhibition, and to the railway village museum (a restored cottage next door) should be included in your exploration. You should also venture as far as Bristol Street and London Street, which run along behind the mechanics institute; here you will see the entrance to the 'tunnel' (now Great Western Business Centre), which gave access from the village to the works for thousands of employees, through the long, bleak wall of the carriage works built in 1868.

Cross Emlyn Square by the pedestrian crossing to the right of the mechanics' institute front entrance, and walk along Oxford Street. Where the railway village ends continue across East Street into Harding Street, and then turn right into Bridge Street.

East Street signals the end of the railway village, and the beginning of Sheppard's Field. John Henry Harding Sheppard was the successful Old Town brewer who gave each of his names to a street in this area around 1870. The terraces of cottages which covered his field have now, for the most part, been cleared, and the site is currently used for surface car parking and an open market. As you walk along Harding Street you will see in front of you the large modern office developments which have recently sprung up between the railway station (to the left), and the shopping centre (to the right). You should also look back, to admire a large mural of a GWR 'King' class engine, executed in 1985.

We have already encountered the southern end of the original Bridge Street (which became Regent Street). Now we are standing at the northern end, which led to the point where the North Wilts Canal, having branched off from the Wilts and Berks, ran beneath the railway lines. Like Regent Street, this part of Bridge Street was built up with terraced housing during the 1850s, and some was later converted to commercial use.

> **Walk along Bridge Street to its junction with Fleet Street and turn left. Cross at the end of Fleet Street by the pedestrian crossing, and walk along on the lower footpath beside Fleming Way, the elevated dual carriageway. When you emerge into the Parade turn left and walk through the pedestrian underpass beneath Fleming Way; then make your way up to the bus stops.**

Fleet Street, of course, takes its name from 'Fleetway', the early track which we encountered further along as Faringdon Road. Like Bridge Street it was built up during the 1850s, and a few early cottages remain. Fleming Way, by contrast, is a relatively modern creation, built in 1958 to divert traffic away from the new shopping centre. It takes its name from Harold Fleming, Swindon Town Football Club's star player between 1907 and 1924, and an England cap. He died in 1955.

Fleming Way follows the line of the North Wilts Canal, which had a long and stormy gestation period before its opening in 1819. It was built to connect the Wilts and Berks Canal with the Thames and Severn, and had the effect of enabling canal traffic to by-pass the supposedly navigable upper reaches of the Thames or Isis, from Lechlade through Oxford to Abingdon. As we saw in chapter three, it was the

existence of these canals which gave Swindon the 'first push' on its way to becoming the large and important town which it is today. And the junction of the North Wilts with the Wilts and Berks Canals, as you stand and wait for your bus back up to Old Town, is precisely under your feet.

At the time of writing (1992) bus no. 11 operates a daytime service to Old Town from Fleming Way every fifteen minutes. If you prefer to walk back up the hill continue along Fleming way, turn right at Whale roundabout into Princes Street. This becomes Clarence Street and then Victoria Road. At the top of Victoria Road turn left into Wood Street, and then right into High Street. From Fleming Way to Old Town Market Square is about a mile, mostly uphill.

The Next Steps

A short book such as this cannot do justice to a subject as large as Swindon. Whole areas of great interest have been entirely omitted, or merely mentioned in passing. But if this book has succeeded in its aim of fuelling your interest in your local history, there are several things which you could do next.

First, there are museums to visit. Thamesdown Borough Council operates four museums, as follows: Swindon Museum, Bath Road (Old Town), includes displays on the archaeology, geology, natural history and social history of the area, and is open without charge daily, 10 a.m. – 6 p.m. (Sunday 2 p.m. – 5 p.m.). The Great Western Railway Museum, Faringdon Road, includes locomotives built at Swindon, and an exhibition depicting the railway's relationship with the town, entitled 'Return to Swindon'; it is open daily, 10 a.m. – 5 p.m. (Sunday 2 p.m. – 5 p.m.). There is an admission charge, which includes entry also to the adjacent Railway Village Museum, a restored foreman's cottage; this has the same opening hours, except that it is closed daily, 1 p.m. – 2 p.m.. At Coate Farm, adjacent to the Coate Water Country Park east of Swindon, there is a museum devoted to the local authors Richard Jefferies and Alfred Williams; this is open at certain weekends. Other local places of interest are Lydiard House and Country Park, west of Swindon, Barbury Castle Country Park, and the Science Museum outstation at Wroughton airfield. Details of these attractions, and all other aspects of local tourism, are available from the Information Centre, Brunel Centre, Swindon SN1 1LN.

Second, there is a local history society to join. The Swindon Society was formed in 1972 to further interest in Swindon, its surroundings and history. It maintains a large collection of historic photographs (some of which have been used in this book), carries out research into Swindon's history, and has regular monthly meetings. It also raises money for local charities. Details may be obtained from the Publicity Officer, Swindon Society, 69 Sandringham Road, Swindon SN3 1HT.

Third, there are other books to read. The published sources for

Swindon's history are to be found in the Local Studies Library which forms part of Swindon Reference Library in Regent Circus. For more advanced research most archival sources relating to Swindon are in the Wiltshire Record Office, Bythesea Road, Trowbridge.

Listed below are the most important published books about the history of Swindon, and these have been heavily used in the writing of the present short history. Other books, relevant to specific topics, are also listed, chapter by chapter.

General

Chandler, C.J., and others, *'Off the map of history'? the development of north-east Wiltshire to 1600*, 1989

Crittall, Elizabeth, and others, *A history of Swindon to 1965*, 1983 [reprinted from the *Victoria History of Wiltshire*, vol. 9, 1970]

Grinsell, L.V., and others, *Studies in the history of Swindon*, 1950 [includes John Betjeman's essay on Swindon architecture]

Jefferies, Richard, *Jefferies' land: a history of Swindon and its environs . . . edited with notes by Grace Toplis*, 1896

Morris, William, *Swindon fifty years ago (more or less): reminiscences, notes and relics of ye old Wiltshire towne*, 1885 [new edition 1970]

Peck, Alan S., *The Great Western at Swindon Works*, 1983

Silto, William, *Of stone and steam: the story of Swindon railway village*, 1989

Chapter One

Anderson, A.S., *The Roman pottery industry in north Wiltshire*, 1979

Arkell, W.J., 'A geological map of Swindon', in *Wiltshire Archaeological and Natural History Magazine*, vol. 52, 1948, pp. 195–212

Burnham, Barry C., and Wacher, John, *The 'small towns' of Roman Britain*, 1990

Gingell, Christopher, 'Excavation of an Iron Age enclosure at Groundwell Farm, Blunsdon St Andrew, 1976–7', in *Wiltshire Archaeological and Natural History Magazine*, vol. 76, 1982, pp. 33–75

Gover, J.E.B., and others, *The place-names of Wiltshire*, 1939 (English Place-Name Society, vol. 16)

Grundy, G.B. 'The Saxon land charters of Wiltshire (first series)',

Archaeological Journal, vol. 76, 1919, pp.143–301 [especially pp. 283–8]

Chapter Two

Aubrey, John, *The natural history of Wiltshire*, 1847

Aubrey, John, and Jackson, J.E. *Wiltshire: the topographical collections*, 1862

Bird, Denis, *The story of Holy Rood: old parish church of Swindon*, 2nd edn., 1991

Britton, John, *The beauties of Wiltshire . . .*, vol. 3, 1825

Burnham and Wacher, 1990 [see above, chapter one]

Canham, Roy, and Phillips, Bernard, *The archaeology of Old Swindon Hill*, no date

Mabbs, A.W. (ed.), *Documents relating to the Goddard family of north Wiltshire*, 2 vols., 1960, 1969

Wiltshire Record Office, 212B/7202A 9a: 1696/7 list of Swindon inhabitants

Chapter Three

Dalby, L.J., *The Wilts and Berks Canal*, 2nd edn., 1986

Delair, J.B., and Dean, Dennis R., 'Gideon Mantell in Wiltshire', in *Wiltshire Archaeological and Natural History Magazine*, vol. 78, 1984, pp. 219–24

Home, Gordon, *The Great Western Railway*, 1913 (Peeps at Great Railways)

MacDermot, E.T., and Clinker, C.R., *History of the Great Western Railway*, vol. 1, 1964

Platt, Alan, *The life and times of Daniel Gooch*, 1987

Chapter Four

Bagley, Philip S., *The transport revolution from 1770*, 1974

Betjeman, John, *First and last loves*, 1952 [includes 'Three churches: St Mark's, Swindon', pp. 185–8]

Burnett, John, *A social history of housing, 1815-1985*, 2nd edn., 1986

Clark, George T., *Report to the General Board of Health on a preliminary inquiry into the sewerage, drainage . . . of the town and parish of Swindon*, 1851

Cockbill, Trevor, *A drift of steam, being a form of 'Who was Who' in New Swindon, Wilts. 1843–1853 . . .*, 1992

Darwin, Bernard, *A century of medical service: the story of the Great Western Railway Medical Fund Society, 1847–1947*, 1947

Large, Frederick, *A Swindon retrospect, 1855–1930*, 1932

MacDermot and Clinker, 1964 [see above, chapter three]

Maggs, Colin G., *Rail centres: Swindon*, 1983

Measom, George, *The illustrated guide to the Great Western Railway*, 1852

Platt, 1987 [see above, chapter three]

Robinson, J.M., *The Wyatts: an architectural dynasty*, 1979

Saint Mark's Swindon 1845–1945: a record of a hundred years' work written by priests and people, 1945

Vaughan, A., *A pictorial record of Great Western architecture*, 1977

Chapter Five

Betjeman, 1952 [see above, chapter four]

——, *John Betjeman's collected poems: enlarged edition*, 1970

Cockbill, Trevor, *Finest thing out: a chronicle of Swindon's torchlit days . . .*, part 1: 1843–1873, 1988

Eversley, D.E.C., 'Engineering and railway works', in *Victoria History of Wiltshire*, vol. 4, 1959, pp. 183–219

Fuller, Frederick, *The railway works and church of New Swindon . . .*, 1987

Jefferies, Richard, *Greene Ferne Farm*, 1880

——, *The hills and the vale*, 1909 [includes 'The story of Swindon', pp. 104–33]

MacDermot and Clinker, 1964 [see above, chapter three]

Maggs, 1983 [see above, chapter four]

Platt, 1987 [see above, chapter three]

Priestley, J.B., *English journey*, 1934

Sheldon, Peter, and Tomkins, Richard, *Roadways: the history of Swindon's street names*, 1979

Silto, J., *A Swindon history, 1840–1901*, 1981

Spencer, F.H., *An inspector's testament*, 1938

Wilson, Roger Burdett (ed.), *Sir Daniel Gooch: memoirs and diary*, 1972

Chapter Six

Burnett, 1986 [see above, chapter four]

Cook, K.J., *Swindon steam, 1921–1951*, 1974

Eversley, 1959 [see above, chapter five]

Harloe, Michael, *Swindon: a town in transition: a study of urban development and overspill policy*, 1975

Hudson, Kenneth, *An awkward size for a town: a study of Swindon at the 100,000 mark*, 1967

Lindley, Kenneth, *Town time and people*, 1962

Maggs, 1983 [see above, chapter four]

Mansbridge, Albert, *The trodden road*, 1940 [chapter on Reuben George, pp. 174–9]

Priestley, 1934 [see above, chapter five]

Sheldon and Tomkins, 1979 [see above, chapter five]

Swindon Expansion Project Joint Steering Committee, *Swindon: a study for further expansion*, 1968 [the 'silver report']

Thamesdown Borough Council, *A new vision for Thamesdown: a consultation document*, 1984

——, *Swindon Railway Village Museum*, no date

Tuckett, Angela, *Up with all that's down! A history of Swindon Trades Council, 1891–1971*, 2nd edn., 1982

Williams, Alfred, *Life in a railway factory*, 1915 [new edn., 1992]

Walking Tour

There have been a number of excellent books of historic photographs of bygone Swindon, compiled by Peter Sheldon, Richard Tomkins, Michael Howell and the Swindon Society, which make the ideal companions for walking tours anywhere in Swindon. See also:

Backhouse, David, *Home brewed*, 1984

Bridgeman, Brian, and others, *Swindon's other railway*, 2nd edn., 1990

Acknowledgements

I am most grateful for their invaluable help to members of staff of Wiltshire County Council, Library and Museum Service, at Swindon and Trowbridge especially Roger Trayhurn, Swindon Reference Librarian, to whom this book is dedicated; to the County Archivist and staff, Wiltshire Record Office; to Brian Bridgeman, Jean Allen and Denis Bird of the Swindon Society who have read the entire text and suggested corrections, as well as supplying illustrations and helping in other ways; to David Buxton and Clare Bishop of Alan Sutton Publishing; and to my wife, Alison, for her encouragement and support.

June 1992   John Chandler
                                                             East Knoyle

Picture Credits

I gratefully acknowledge the following for kindly lending me, or permitting me to copy, illustrations: Swindon Society and Denis Bird: (page nos.) 21, 24, 26, 45, 52 (bottom), 58, 64, 74, 82, 88, 89, 90, 92, 94, 96, 97, 99, 101 (both), 103 (top), 105, 106, 107, 110 (top); Wiltshire County Council Library & Museum Service – Archaeology & Museum Section (Roy Canham): 4, 11, 15; – Headquarters Local Studies Library: 31, 36, 46, 51; – Swindon Reference Library: 28 (P16095), 29 (P16090), 32 (P16089), 35 (P18118), 38 (P18110), 44 (bottom), 50, 52 (top, P17965), 53 (P17963), 60 (P17984), 70 (P17987), 72 (P16093), 73 (P16092), 79 (P31223), 93 (P17983); Wiltshire Record Office: 17, 18, 19, 37, 62 (both), 63, 69, 100. The sources of other illustrations are: author (taken summer 1992): 1, 23, 33, 47, 55, 65, 66, 76, 77, 81, 83 (both), 84, 85, 103 (bottom), 104 (both), 108, 110 (bottom); Crittall, 1983 (see bibliography p. 113): 71; Jefferies, 1896 (see p. 113): 69; Measom, 1852 (see p. 115): 40, 41, 42; Spencer, 1938 (see p. 115): 61; plan of GWR works 1846 and 1935: 44 (top), 75.

Index

Note: Some street and personal names, mentioned only in passing, have been omitted.

agriculture, 2, 4–6, 10–13, 29, 59
Albert Street, 54, 95
alehouses, *see* inns
Anderson, Alexander, 93
Apsley House, 32, 95
Ashton Keynes, 5
Aubrey, John, 18, 20, 27

Badbury, 7, 8; Wick, 10
'Barracks', 53, 65, 106, 108
Bath, 34, 38, 39, 54, 92, 95, 105;
    Road, 32–3, 67, 95–7
Bell Hotel, 22, 91
Bertram, T.H., 43
Betjeman, Sir John, 22, 31, 51,
    59–60, 67, 68, 77, 93, 94
Binyon, Brightwen, 102
Blackford family, 92
Blagrove, 9
Blunsdon, 1, 9, 10
borough council, 57, 78, 80, 85, 102,
    105
Bowley, Richard, 91
Box Tunnel, 34, 38, 48
Braydon Forest, 1, 22
brickmaking, 30
Bridge Street, 65, 73, 102, 109
Bridges, 30, 32; *see also* named
    bridges
Bristol, 32, 34, 38, 39, 105
Britannia Place, 17, 32, 54
Britton, John, 14, 25, 27, 30
Broad Street, 67, 80
Brock Hill (Cricklade Street), 22–3,
    92–4, 95
Broome, 2, 12, 14, 20
Brunel Centre and Plaza, 84-5, 104,
    106, 110–11
Brunel, Isambard K., 27, 32, 34,
    37–8, 42, 43, 48
Buckworth, Cambs., 94
builders; *see* housebuilding

building socieites, 63, 106
Burderop Down, 4
business parks and offices, 80–1, 109

Cambria Bridge and Place, 30, 65,
    106
Canal Walk, 30, 84–5, 104
canals, 27–30, 32, 37, 39, 64–5, 85,
    104–6, 109, 111
carriage works, 58, 73, 108; *see also*
    railway works
Cennick, John, 25
Cetus Buildings, 65
Chaddington, 9, 28
chapels, *see* nonconformity
Cheltenham, 54, 92; branch, 34, 36–9,
    45
Chippenham, 39
Chiseldon, 2, 7, 8, 10, 80
churches: Christ Church, 69, 90, 93–4;
    Holy Rood, 16, 69, 90; St
    Mark's, 45, 50–1, 106–7
Churchward, G.J., 73, 75, 79
coal, 29, 38, 39
Coate, 14, 69; reservoir, 28, 106
Cobbett, William, 32
Collett, C.B., 75, 77
Commercial Road, 30, 67, 68, 102
corn exchange, 54–5, 88
Covingham, 5, 85; *see also*
    Durocornovium
Crewe, 41, 47
Cricklade, 2, 22; Street (Brock Hill),
    22–3, 92–4, 95

Dammas Lane, 88
Deacon Street, 60
Devizes Road, 17, 25, 32, 95
Domesday Book, 9–10
Dorcan, 5, 85
Dover Street, 66–7
Drove Road, 36

Dunsford, William, 29, 32
Durocornovium, 5–7, 14, 15

Eastcott, 9, 11–13, 20–2, 28, 37,
    99, 102; Farm, 30, 99; Hill,
    54, 65, 67, 95, 99–100; Road,
    99–100; *see also* Upper
    Eastcott Farm
education, see mechanics' institute;
    schools; Workers' Educational
    Association
Elcombe, 1
Eldene, 10, 85
electricity supply, 73
Ellendun, 8
Emlyn Square, 48, 72, 107–8
Ermin Street, 5
Even Swindon, 9, 11, 31, 67, 80, 82

factories, 59, 78–9, 80; *see also*
    carriage works; railway works
Faringdon Road, 106, 109
farming, *see* agriculture
Fleet, and Fleet Street, 64, 73, 106,
    109–11
Fleming, Harold, 109
Fleming Way, 30, 32, 105, 109,
    111
football, 73, 109
Freshbrook, 1

gas supply, 70
geology, 2–4, 9, 26–7
George, Reuben, 78, 79
Gibbs, C.H., 50
Gluepot Inn, 108
Goddard, Ambrose, 36, 39, 93;
    Pleydell, 25; Thomas (*fl.*
    1697), 20–1; Thomas (*fl.*
    1764), 25; family, 16–18, 20,
    25, 90
Goddard Arms Inn, 21, 54, 92
Golden Lion Bridge, 30, 64, 65,
    102, 105; Inn, 50, 64, 65, 104
Gooch, Daniel, 37–40, 43, 46, 49,
    51, 57–8
Gorse Hill, 62, 67, 80
Great Western Railway, 32, 34–5,
    38–40, 41–3, 45–51, 76, 78;

Park, 51, 106–7; *see also* rail-
    ways, etc.
Greenbridge, 83
Groundwell, 4, 8, 11

Hall, James, 72
Hay Lane, 34
Haydon, 9, 85; Wick, 7, 10
health, 49, 51, 54, 70–1
High Street, 16, 22, 87, 91, 95
Highworth, 18, 22, 31, 32, 87
housebuilding: nineteenth-century,
    59–68, 99–100, 102; twentieth-
    century, 80–5
Hudson, Kenneth, 77, 85

industries, *see* carriage works; fact-
    ories; railway works
inns, 20, 21–2, 70, 73; *see also* named
    inns
Iron Age, 4–5

Jefferies, Richard, 28, 37, 38, 53,
    69–70, 71, 90, 92, 95
Job, Zephaniah, 50
John, David Murray, 78, 85

kilns, 6
Kingsdown, 9
Kingshill, 62, 67, 80

Latton, 28
Lawn: (gardens) 27, 83, 89–91; (housing
    estate) 83, 90; (mansion) 16, 89–90
Lechlade, 18, 28, 109
Liddington, 9; Wick, 10
Liden, 85
Little London, 24, 32, 94, 95
local government, 67, 70–1, 80, 83, 85,
    102
Lydiard: (both) 8, 9; Millicent, 10

'Magic Roundabout', 30
Manchester Road, 30, 63, 67
Mannington, 8, 9, 11
manors, 9–10, 12–13, 67
mansio, 5
Mantell, George, 25–6; Gideon, 25–7,
    32, 34, 35, 40, 91

markets: New Swindon, 51, 67, 73; Old Swindon (and market place, market house) 16–18, 22, 25, 29, 54, 87–9, 91
Marlborough, 22, 50
Measom, George, 41, 42
mechanics' institute, 51–3, 72, 73, 108
medical fund society, 51
medieval period, 9–12, 16–17, 95
mill, 16, 89
Moredon, 7–8, 9, 11, 83
Morris, William, 24, 28–9, 30, 35
Mouldon, 9
mural paintings, 77, 99, 109
museums, 32, 53, 72, 95, 108, 112

Nethercott, 9, 10, 12–13
Newport Street, 17, 24–6, 87
newspapers, 73
nonconformity, 25–6, 49–50, 53, 65, 70, 73, 96, 100–2, 106
North Street, 100
Nythe, 9, 85; Farm, 39

offices and business parks, 80–1, 109
Okus, 14, 80; see also quarries
Oxford, 58, 79

Parade, 30, 32, 104–5
parishes, 9
Park, 83, 90
Passmore, Arthur, 14
Penhill, 7, 8, 83
Pinehurst, 7, 82
place-names, 5, 8–9
Planks, 89, 96
planning, town, 79–80, 83, 85
population, 1, 11–12, 20–1, 31, 46, 54, 82–3, 85
Powell, James 'Raggy', 78, 79
prehistory, 4–5, 14
Priestley, J.B., 64, 76–7
Princes Street, 30
Prospect Hill and Place, 32, 54, 67, 95
Purton, 1, 7

quarries, 12, 15, 18–20, 22, 25, 27, 29–30, 54, 59, 80, 97–8
Queens: Drive, 83; Park, 14

railway, 27, 30, 34–40, 73, 98–9; gauge, 40, 43; locomotives, 38, 39, 40, 43, 45, 52–3, 57–9, 74–7, 109; refreshment rooms, 39–43; station, 34, 39–40, 42, 63; village, 30, 40, 47–51, 64, 72, 107–9; works, 30, 37–9, 43–6, 57–9, 65, 73–8, 80, 85, 98; see also carriage works; Cheltenham branch; Great Western Railway
Ray, River, 7, 27
Redcliffe Street, 82
Regent Circus, 60, 65, 67, 71, 102; Street, 30, 65, 67, 100–5, 109
Rhinoceros Inn, 95
Rigby, J. & C., 42–3, 46, 48–9
roads and road travel, 21–2, 25, 27, 80, 85, 92; see also Roman roads; trams
Rodbourne Cheney, 9, 82; Stream, 7
Roman period, 5–7, 14–16, 18; kilns, 6; roads, 5, 15

Salisbury, 38
Saxon period, 7–9, 15, 91; boundaries, 7–8; huts, 15–16, 88
schools, 25–7, 49, 50–1, 70, 73
Scott, Sir George Gilbert, 93
Semington, 28, 104
Sevenhampton, 18
Shaw, 6, 9
Sheppard, John H.H., 61–2, 65, 91, 109
shops and shopping, 54, 70, 73, 92, 102–5; see also trade
smuggling, 25
Snell, Edward, 45, 49–50
South Marston, 9, 28
Sparcells, 9
Spencer, F.H., 60–2, 69–70, 102
Stanton Fitzwarren, 7
Strange family, 25, 27
Stratton St Margaret, 1, 5, 9, 10, 80, 82, 85
Sturrock, Archibald, 43, 45, 46
suburbs, 80, 82–3, 85

Thamesdown Borough Council, 77
theatre, 73, 85
Thompson, Henry, 21
tithe map, 37, 62, 68
Toothill, 1, 6, 9
town gardens, 19, 75, 97–8; hall, 67, 70, 71, 102
trade, 29; *see also* shops and shopping; *and* named trades
tradesmen, 21, 22, 59
trams, 73, 74
'trip', 51–3

Union Row, 54
Unwin, Raymond, 82
Upper Eastcott Farm, 60, 62, 65, 99; *see also* Eastcott

Victoria Road and Street, 54, 67, 68–9, 95, 99
Vilett family, 21, 22, 51, 93; estate, 63, 67, 68
Wadard, 10

Walcot, 5, 11, 12, 20, 83, 90
Wanborough, 8, 10; *see also Durocornovium*
water supply, 38, 49, 54, 56, 71
West Swindon, 1, 6, 11, 83, 85
Westcott, 9, 11, 12; Farm, 30; Place, 64, 65
Western Street, 80–1
Westleaze, 11–12
Whale Bridge, 30; Inn, 65
Wheeler, Betty, 27
Whitehead, George, 62
Wick Farm, 10
Williams, Alfred, 78
windmills, 80, 92
Wolverton, Bucks., 49, 47
women, employment of, 59, 79
Wood Street, 16, 22, 24, 32, 87, 92, 95, 96
Wotton Bassett, 22, 27, 31, 32
Workers' Educational Association, 78
Wroughton, 1, 2, 8, 9, 12, 31, 71
Wyatt, Sir Matthew Digby, 48